ETTORE MAIOTTI

The Painting the Nude Handbook

Learning from the Masters

Clarkson Potter/Publishers
New York

To Carol Southern

Published by Clarkson N. Potter, Inc., 201 East 50th Street, New York, New York, 10022, and distributed by Crown Publishers, Inc. Member of the Crown Publishing Group

Originally published in Italy by Gruppo Editoriale Fabbri, S.p.A., Milan
Copyright © 1991 by Gruppo Editoriale Fabbri, Bompiani, Sonzogno, Etas, S.p.A., Milan. English translation © 1991 by Gruppo Editoriale Fabbri, S.p.A., Milan

Translated by Terrence Rogers

Those works not otherwise cited are those of Ettore Maiotti

Photo Credits:
Bardazzi (p. 152)
Scala, Florence (p. 153)

© SIAE, Rome, 1991, for the works by Felice Casorati, Nicolas de Staël, František Kupka, Henri Matisse, Piet Mondrian, Félix Vallotton, Maurice de Vlaminck

CLARKSON N. POTTER, POTTER and colophon are trademarks of Clarkson N. Potter, Inc.

Printed in Italy by Gruppo Editoriale Fabbri, S.p.A., Milan

Library of Congress Cataloging in Publication Data

Maiotti, Ettore.
Painting the nude: learning from the masters / Ettore Maiotti.
p. cm.

1. Nude in art. 2. Painting-Technique. I Title.
ND 1290. 5. M35   1991
751. 4-dc20   91-8382
                                                                      CIP

ISBN: 0-517-58592-8
10 9 8 7 6 5 4 3 2 1

First American Edition

CONTENTS

INTRODUCTION

Each time I sit down to write the introduction to one of my handbooks, and there are quite a few of them now, my mind goes back to my art school days. Perhaps because I was very young and headstrong, with a burning desire to express what I felt inside me, and the school, in my opinion, never gave me a chance to do so, or perhaps merely because young people are always anxious to "cut corners", the fact is that I very often found myself in conflict with the authorities.

On November 21, 1966, I was expelled from the Art School in Milan with this letter:

"I wish to inform you that as of today you are expelled from this school, for the following reasons:
1) Failure to abide by the syllabus jointly established by the headmaster and the Teaching Staff;
2) Openly argumentative attitude towards your Teacher;
3) Provocative influence on your classmates."

This happened during my fourth year at school. During the previous years I had won several medals. Of course, due to my unruly behaviour, I was always awarded the second or third prizes and never the first! But really I was a good student from a scholastic point of view: it was just that my behaviour was not always what it should have been.

However, there was another reason for my expulsion. There were changes at the top of the school. The new headmaster, for reasons unknown to me, replaced our fresco teacher, an extraordinarily clever and gifted artist, with a really second-rate teacher. We students of the fresco section rebelled. I was chosen to represent the class, and the inevitable happened. The whole school went on strike. I was never allowed back. The fresco section was closed down.

Together with some of my classmates who had opted not to go back to school, we rented a studio in a tumble-down old house in a working class area of old Milan. This decision was made purposely so as not to abandon fresco painting and "to keep our hands in".

The main problem was how to manage to paint nudes. At school there were models who sat for us twice a week. The place was heated and comfortable. But now? We obviously didn't have much money and what we did have practically all went to pay the rent. My wife, who at that time was my fiancée, was the only one of us who had a job, and I was very dependent on her earnings. She was the mainstay of the whole group. We had no money to splash out on models, and the models certainly had no intention of sitting for a band of penniless, young art students without at least getting paid for it.

However, in the area where we had rented our studio, which was inhabited for the most part by prostitutes, immigrants, pickpockets and the unemployed, we were shown enormous solidarity. A warmth and humanity that I often think about with nostalgia and that I shall cherish forever.

When they got to know us and learned about the school and about how anxious we were to paint and how we were bursting with ideas, enthusiasm and hunger, they did not hesitate to rally round us. They even invited us to dinner a few times. And out of those humble kitchens came forth spaghetti dinners and wine such as I have never tasted since.

When they learned that we had no money to pay for models, a sort of bond of brotherhood was formed. They almost fell over one another to drop by at our studio. The first one, I remember quite clearly, was the concierge. A huge lady of around fifty. She was tall and weighed about 200 pounds. The funniest thing was listening to the comments when the drawings were completed. Because in the end everyone in the house dropped in to the studio. I have never since seen people become so excited about anything. Next it was the turn of a prostitute, followed by a cook, an ex-boxer and even the barman's wife. It became a habit for these people to drop in at the studio and sit for us. It didn't make any difference whether they were naked or clothed. For them it was a way of getting together for a chat or to talk about their lives full of misfortunes or ruined by alcohol. They were disarmingly unselfish and full of fellow feeling, always ready to give one another a hand.

The years went by; the house was sold and modernized. Every so often I still happen to pass through that part of town. Now, the area is inhabited by "the elite". And so I recall the words written by the poet Luciano Roncalli who knew us during that period: "The place reverberated with unspeakable human grief and pain, the toil, the weariness of millions of wretched anonymous footsteps up and down those dim staircases; the slow progressive crumbling of youthful dreams up and down dim staircases."

I dedicate this book to my fellow students, to my studio companions, to my wife and to those nameless models who by their solidarity and human kindness enabled me to go on studying to become a painter. They also gave me the strength to go on and to learn how to sacrifice myself for my painting. There is still something of that past in each of my paintings and I consider myself fortunate to have had that experience: at a time when perhaps I could have given up the idea of becoming a painter I found so many outstretched hands that I will never forget.

THE HUMAN FIGURE AND ITS PROPORTIONS

The basic unit of measurement for everything constructed by man is the human figure, and the basic unit used to construct the human figure is the head. This has not always been so, however: the ancient Egyptians, for example, used the length of the middle finger as their unit of measurement, so that the Egyptian statue on the right can be divided into twenty-one and a half equal parts, headgear included (nineteen parts for the figure and two and a half for the headgear).

It seems probable that the same rule was also used by the Greeks. The Greeks, however, with their love of beauty and "divine" perfection, studied the subject of proportion in greater depth. Myron, Phidias and Polycletus of Argos were the most famous trio of sculptors during the fifth century B.C. Polycletus's statue of *Doryphoros*, for example (of which there is a copy in the Museum of Naples), possesses perfect proportions.

The *Doryphoros* is the statue of a warrior (pre-

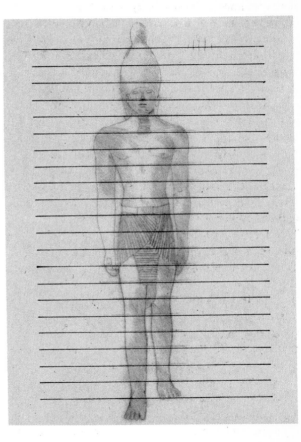

Egyptian canon

7

sumably Achilles) holding a lance in his left hand. It was known as "Kanon" (i.e. canon or standard) since it was to serve as the basis for all future studies of the human figure. *Kanon* was also the title of the essay Polycletus wrote about the statue.

What is new about the *Doryphoros* is not so much the fact that Polycletus used the width of the hand at the base of the fingers as his unit of measurement (since this is practically the same as the length of the middle finger) as the way in which

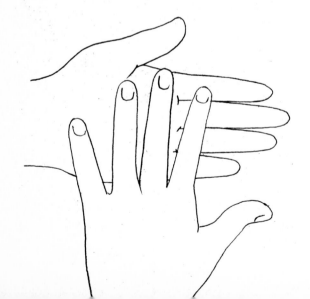

the unit of measurement is applied. The Egyptian figure is static, almost a symbol, whereas the Greek statue reflects movement, attitude and dynamic force: in a word, realism.

The Vitruvian Figure

The canon or standard used is still the same. We can see this by examining Lysippus's canon handed down to us by Vitruvius. The basic unit is the length of the head, measured from the point of the chin to the top of the skull. Note that this is two and a half times the length of the middle finger.

Let us take a closer look at the rule. The face can be divided into three equal parts: the first part is from the point of the chin to the base of the nose; the second from the base to the root of the nose; the third from the root of the nose to the roots of the hair.

The length of the face, from the chin to the roots of the hair, is one-tenth the length of the body. The total length of the head is one-eighth the length of the body from the soles of the feet to the top of the skull. The distance between the top of the skull and the fork of the breastbone corresponds to the length of the foot and is one-sixth the length of the body. The centre of the human

8

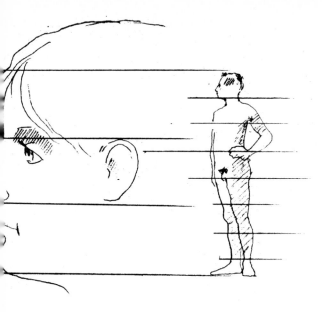

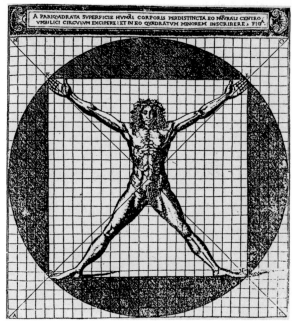

On the right: Caesarian: Vitruvian Figure

body is the navel. The height of the whole body is equal to the length of the arms outstretched in the form of a cross.

The "Vitruvian figure" has been handed down to us by the Roman architect and essayist Caesarian who believed that it was possible to "proportion every earthly thing" through the human figure. Caesarian has left us an important drawing which

helps us to understand the canons of the Renaissance.

Lysippus's canon was followed throughout the Renaissance period. In his treatise on painting, written in the 14th century, the Florentine artist Cennino Cennini had this to say about what he called "the proportions of the perfect human body":

9

"Before I go any further I want to speak about the proportions of a man's body. I will not speak about the female body because there are no perfect proportions.

First, as I said before, the face is divided into three equal measures: the head is one, the nose the other and from the nose to the chin the other. The distance from the root of the nose to the end of the eye is the same as one of these three measures; from the end of the eye to the ear, another. The distance from one ear to the other is the same as the length of one face; from underneath the chin to the start of the throat, one of three measures; the throat itself, one measure; from the fork of the throat to the top of the shoulder, one face; from the shoulder to the elbow, one face; from the elbow to the wrist, one face and one of the three measures; the length of the whole hand, one face; from the fork of the throat to the fork of the stomach, one face; from the stomach to the navel, one face; from the navel to the hip, one face; from the hip to the knee, two faces; from the knee to the heel, two faces; from the heel to the sole, one of the three measures; the length of the foot, one face.

Man is as tall as the length of his arms outstretched, and crosswise from the tips of his fingers to halfway down his thigh. Man's height is equal to eight faces and two of the three measures. Man has one rib less than woman on the left side of his chest. The bones of his whole body should be visible. Of his masculine attributes, his penis should be of such a size as pleases women and his testicles should be small, well shaped and youthful. To be beautiful, man should be dark-skinned and woman fair-skinned.

I shall not discuss the measurements of irrational animals because there is no one measurement for them all. Draw and sketch as many of them as you can from real life and you will see. This is the only way to learn."

Leonardo da Vinci accepted Vitruvius's method of measuring. He drew a figure with outstretched arms inside a square. He also adopted the rule of the head being equal to the eighth part of the overall height of the body. This rule is valid for individuals taller than 1 m 85 cm, while for people shorter than 1 m 80 cm, the body is equal to seven and a half times the length of the head.

In 1577, in his *Dialogue on Painting*, Lodovico Dolce published the rules for the measurement of the human figure:

"The head, or rather the face, is divided into three parts: one from the roots of the hair to the eyebrows; the other from the eyebrows to the end of the nostrils; the last from the nostrils to the chin.

Leonardo da Vinci (1452-1519): A Study of Proportions –
Gallerie dell'Accademia, Venice

The first is considered to be the seat of wisdom; the second, of beauty; the third, of goodness. Therefore, the human body is made up of ten heads according to some, and according to others, nine, eight and even seven. Authors of great renown have written that man cannot grow taller than seven feet; and the foot measures sixteen fingers; and the centre of the human body is naturally the navel. Therefore, when man stands with his arms outstretched, by drawing lines from the navel to the soles of the feet, and to the tips of the fingers, he forms a perfect circle.

The eyebrows joined together form both the circles of the eyes; the semicircles of the ears must be the same size as the open mouth; the width of the nose above the mouth, the same as the length of the eye. The nose is as long as the width of the lips; the distance between one eye and the other is the same as the length of the eye itself; the distance between the ear and the nose is the same as the length of the middle finger. The hand should be as long as the face. The arm is two and a half times the thickness of the finger. The thigh is one and a half times as thick as the arm.

I shall explain the length in greater detail. From the top of the head to the tip of the nose is one face, and from the tip of the nose to the fork-shaped bone at the top of the chest, is the second, and from the top of the chest to the pit of the stomach is the third; from the latter to the navel is the fourth, and from the navel to the genital organs the fifth, which is precisely exactly half the length of the body, not counting the head.

Then, from the thigh down to the knee is two faces, and from the knee to the sole of the foot the other three. The length of the arm is three faces, starting from the ligament of the shoulder down to the wrist. The distance from the heel to the instep is the same as the distance from the instep to the tips of the toes. Man's body, measured around the chest under the arm pits, is exactly half as broad as it is long."

Modern Canons

Modern canons basically reflect the canon of Lysippus except for a few minor variations as far as details are concerned. The head, from the top of the skull to the base of the chin, however, still remains the unit of measurement and is divided into four equal parts. The first part starts at the top of the head and goes down to the roots of the hair; the second goes from the roots of the hair to the eyebrows; the third from the eyebrows to the base of the nose; the fourth from the base of the nose to the base of the chin. Adding a fifth part to the base of the chin gives us the measurement of the neck. If we divide the strip from the eyebrows to the base of the nose vertically into five parts, we can see that the second part and the fourth part are occupied by the eyes. We can also divide the width of the eye into three parts: one is occupied by the pupil.

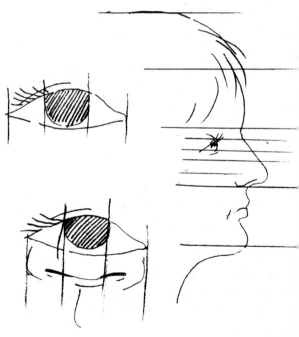

Consequently, the opening of the eye is equal to one-third of its width. The nose is as wide at the nostrils as the measurement of one eye. The mouth is as wide as the distance between the pupils or, in other words, one eye and a half. The ears measure the same as the distance between the line of the eye and the base of the nose.

The figure is always divided into seven and a half parts, with a difference as far as the female figure is concerned; modern canons have in fact stipulated more precise measurements. The height is seven measures (compared to the male figure); the span of the arms is slightly less than the length of the body (while in man it is exactly the same). The torso is also different: men are broader on the upper part of the torso and women on the lower part (because of their more highly developed hips).

I have noted a considerable increase in the height of women belonging to the last few generations, and I am consequently examining the possiblity of considering their height to be equal to seven and a half times that of the head. It goes without saying that this rule must be adapted to suit the figure in question and is used exclusively as a base for construction.

Fritsch's Canon

In order to paint a figure properly, it is necessary to be acquainted with at least one of the canons of construction.

The most modern and practical canon for a beginner is the one devised by Schmidt (1849) and perfected by Fritsch (1895), from whom it takes its name.

This canon contemplates man viewed from the front, standing as if at attention. The basic module is defined by the base of the nose and the top edge of the pubic bones. The segment NP joining these two points is divided into four equal parts: Nb, bc, cO, and OP. If a segment equal to one of these four is added above the point N, the size of the head is obtained. If a line of the same length is drawn to the right and to the left of point b, we get points S and S' which give the width of the shoulders.

From points S and S' we then draw two cross segments through point N to obtain points d and d' which correspond to the width of the head.

If we now draw a line parallel to SS' through point P of the same length as dd', we get points A and A', the position of the joints of the legs. When we join A to S' and A' to S, the point at which the lines intersect is point O or the navel.

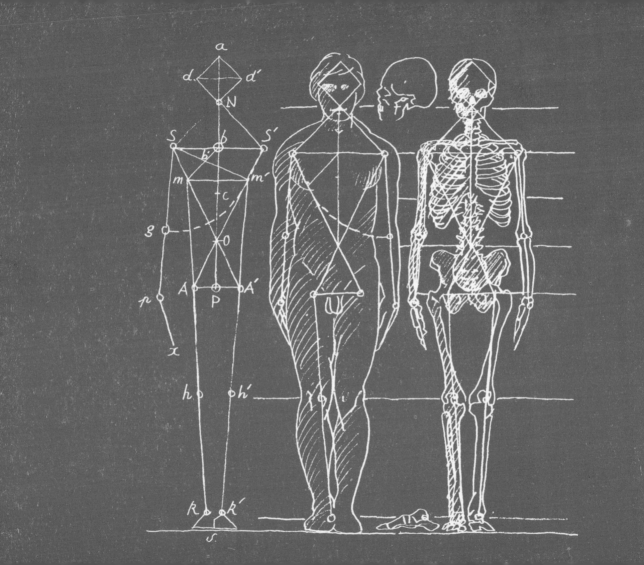

From point *b* we draw a line parallel to *Sd'* to get point *m*; from *m* a line parallel to *SS'* gives us *m'*. The two points *m* and *m'* indicate the positions of the nipples.

The length of *Sm'* is the length of the upper arm and the distance between the nipple and the navel (*mO*) is the length of the forearm. The distance between the navel and one of the hip joints (*OA*) is the length of one hand.

Ah, the length of the thigh, is equal to *mA* and *hk*, the length of the leg below the knee, is equal to *mA'*. The height of the foot is one quarter the length of the head.

These rules are extremely practical and original: if we superimpose the pattern on the human skeleton we see how it can also be applied to the bone structure. The rules must always be kept in mind when drawing the human figure.

In past centuries the rules were associated with deeper, more spiritual matters than they are now. The rules were in any case meant as an aid to imaginative expression, not as a restraint. The basic module used for the construction of the figure was chosen for its symbolic value. When man became aware of the importance of thought and his ability to reason, which made him similar to the Gods, he chose the head as the basic unit of measurement to replace the hand, which symbolized manual work.

This is not the place to go more deeply into this complicated subject, but a few brief remarks will demonstrate how much importance was attached to the idea of the module as a symbol.

Look carefully at the figure shown on page 16.

Several of the writings of the neoplatonic philosopher Francesco Di Giorgio were devoted to the rules of mystical geometry. In the visible world, according to Di Giorgio, the invisible and mental relationship between the soul and God is revealed through the body. The human figure can therefore be applied to all the functions upheld by the relationship. The plan of the church shown in the figure is thus deliberately anthropomorphic.

Fritsch's Canon

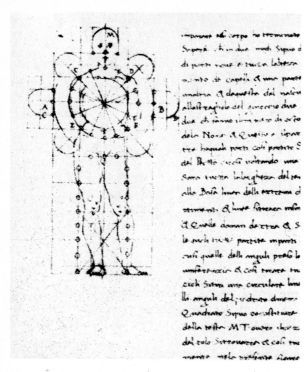

Sketch of the Plan of a Church, *from De Harmonia Mundi totius by Francesco di Giorgio – Venice, 1525*

On the right: a summary chart of the proportions of the various parts of the body

The "Inaccuracies" of the Masters

After practising the rules we have described so far and "getting an eye" for correct proportions, you may well find when you visit exhibitions and museums that some of the human figures painted by great artists are inexplicably "wrongly" proportioned. The reason for this is often the way in which the work is exhibited. Originally, in fact, many paintings and frescoes were situated very high up in churches and the like. The artists therefore calculated their "inaccurate" proportions in such a way that they would be perfect only when seen from below. We can take Michelangelo's famous sculpture of *David* as an example of this. If we look at photographs of the statue in a book, we will immediately notice that the head is out of proportion with the rest of the body. But this only happens when the photograph is taken at the same height as the statue. If we look at the statue from below the pedestal, as it was intended to be seen, we find that the proportions are perfect.

Paintings in exhibitions may be hung wrongly, either because the walls are not high enough or simply because not enough care has been taken. In such cases we should try to look at the painting from the lowest position possible. Bend down low, or, if you are not worried about what other people may think, lie flat on the floor. I have done this many times and, as you can well imagine, some of the scenes that ensued were worthy of inclusion in an anthology of comedy.

To sum up briefly what we have said so far, observe how in these drawings the proportions are given by the height of the head.

Leonardo da Vinci and His Pupils

Leonardo was born on April 15, 1452 at Anchiano near Vinci in the province of Florence. He was the illegitimate son of the notary Piero da Vinci. When he was seventeen, his father sent him to work in Andrea del Verrocchio's studio. In a letter in the *Codice Atlantico* dated 1482 and addressed to Ludovico il Moro, Duke of Milan, Leonardo offers his services for implements of war, engineering works, architecture and stage design. He remained in Milan from 1483 to 1499 working on a project for an equestrian statue of Francesco Sforza. The fall of the Sforza Dukedom prevented the statue from being completed. In 1483 he was commissioned to paint the *Madonna of the Rocks*, of which two signed versions exist, one in the National Gallery in London and the other in the Louvre. Documents also bear witness to commis-

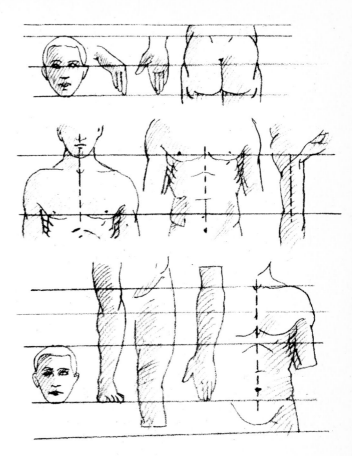

sions for other important works such as the *Last Supper* in the refectory of the monastery of Santa Maria delle Grazie (Milan) and the decorations for rooms in the Sforza Castle in Milan. With the fall of the Sforzas in 1500, Leonardo moved to Mantua. Here he drew the cartoon of Isabella d'Este, now in the Louvre. In 1503 he was commissioned by the Lords of Florence to decorate the walls of the Council Chamber with a fresco devoted to the *Battle of Anghiari*: the work was never carried out, however, and not even the cartoon has survived. In 1506 he was called back to Milan by the French Governor Charles d'Amboise and remained there until 1513, when he went to Rome to work for Giuliano de' Medici, the brother of Pope Leo X. It is known that in Rome he painted a *Madonna with Child* and other paintings that have since been lost. In 1516 he moved to Amboise in France and the paintings in his studio there included the *Mona Lisa* and *S. Anne*. He died in Cloux on May 2, 1519.

Leonardo da Vinci is famous for his constant quest for perfection. In his famous book on Leonardo, Solmi mentions a remark made by the artist himself: "Man has an inborn tendency to reproduce himself in his works and to search for reflections of his own nature in living creatures and objects; this is why there is an endless variety of tastes. Just as God created Man in His own image, so the painter creates figures which always bear his own likeness. I have known some painters who appear always to draw self-portraits. This is an error the artist must take care not to make."

Following Leonardo's logic, perfection is reached only by repeating the same model many times until the number of errors is reduced to a reasonable minimum. Perfection, however, has no limits and the word reasonable is open to many interpretations: it follows that there will always be room for improvement.

In any case, the first thing to do is to find the most expressive position for the subject by trying again and again, leaving the details until later.

Every little detail must be in harmony with the general movement of the body. The position of the hand must correspond to the general position of the arm and the position of the arm implies the position of the body. The eye of the observer must be able to scan the whole of the picture without being disturbed in any way, like a bird of prey in flight. Everything must be harmony and continuity, with no sudden or unexpected movements.

The personality and great skill of Leonardo da Vinci set a model for his pupils to follow. They were fascinated by certain small touches that

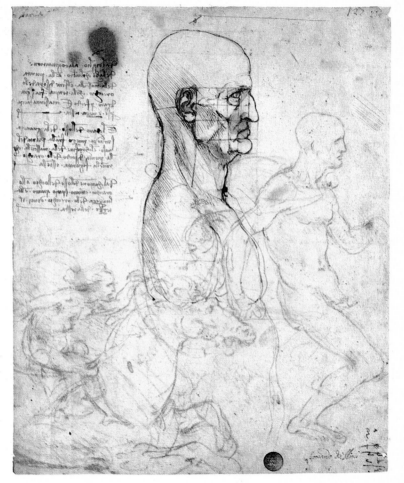

Leonardo da Vinci: A Study of Proportions
(ca. 1490-1494) and Study for the Battle of
Anghiari *(ca. 1503-1504) –*
Gallerie dell'Accademia, Venice

19

Leonardo da Vinci:
The Last Supper
(detail) – Church of
Santa Maria delle
Grazie, Refectory,
Milan

only their master could create. An example of this is given by carefully observing the left hand of the Apostle James in the *Last Supper*.

The hand was studied by Cesare da Sesto, one of Leonardo's pupils, and we find it again in the same position in a later painting done by Cesare da Sesto himself.

Cesare da Sesto is known as one of the many Lombard disciples of Leonardo da Vinci and, according to Vasari, one of the best. More recent critics have confirmed this positive judgement and have also shown how his style was not totally dependent on the teachings of Leonardo. Little is known about his life, and since none of his works can be dated, it is difficult to establish any kind of chronological sequence. Though nothing is known about his formative years it is very probable that he worked with Leonardo da Vinci. Between 1500 and 1510 it would appear that Cesare lived in Rome since Vasari mentions that a "Cesare from Milan" worked with Peruzzi at Ostia. The contact with the elegant classicism of Peruzzi seems to have been highly influential since in the works carried out after his return to Milan, plastic beauty combines with an atmosphere similar to that of Leonardo. Examples are the *Madonna with Child and Lamb* (Poldi Pezzoli Museum, Milan), a free adaptation of Leonardo's *S. Anne and the Virgin* now in the Louvre, *S. Jerome*, belonging to the Cook Collection, and the large *Baptism of Christ*. In about 1514 Cesare moved to the South of Italy where he worked until 1520, mostly between Naples and Messina. This is documented by the large *Adoration of the Magi* (Naples Gallery) and the *Madonna with SS. George and John the Baptist*, both of which are explicit references to Raphael, and the works carried out on his return to Milan such as the *Polyptych of S. Rocco* (Sforza Castle Museum, Milan). The polyptych, which is one of his finest works, was commissioned in 1523. Only six of the fourteen panels were completed, suggesting that the work was interrupted by the artist's death.

Young painters have always followed one of the masters. Just as Leonardo's pupils studied Leonardo, so Michelangelo studied Masaccio and made sketches of the figures in the Cappella Brancacci and Caravaggio was influenced by Lorenzo Lotto, Savoldo, Moretto and the Campi family. During all historical and artistic periods all great artists have started by following the example set by other artists as great as themselves.

Degas, for example, wished to emulate the skill of Ingres. In one of his essays on art, Baudelaire wrote: "In Paris there are only two men who can draw as excellently as Delacroix; one of these has

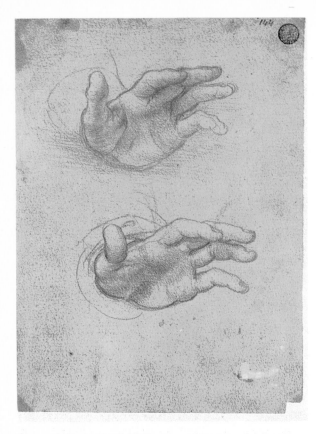

Cesare da Sesto (1477-1523): Copy of Study by Leonardo da Vinci for the Left Hand of the Apostle James in the Last Supper – *Gallerie dell'Accademia, Venice*

Cesare da Sesto: Madonna with Children Playing – *Gallarati Scotti Collection*

a technique similar to that of Delacroix himself, while the other's is completely in contrast. The first is Daumier, the caricaturist, and the second is Ingres, the great painter who admired Raphael so much. These remarks may surprise both friends and enemies, both allies and opponents. But a careful analysis of the works of these great artists shows that they have in common the ability to depict the aspect of nature they wish to represent in a formally perfect and complete manner.

Daumier perhaps draws better than Delacroix, especially if pure skill is put before the amazing abilities of a great genius suffering from his own geniality. Ingres, with the attention he pays to detail, perhaps draws better than either of the other two, if we put the skilful elegance of the details before the harmony of the whole or the nature of each fragment before the nature of the composition. We must learn to love all three of them ...."

Jean-Auguste-Dominique Ingres

At the age of seventeen, after several years of study at the Academy of Toulouse, Ingres entered David's "atelier", where he was taught in the classical tradition.

In 1806, after winning the Prix de Rome, he went to Italy and was to stay until 1824, reacting perhaps against the lack of enthusiasm with which his works were received in France. He was back in Rome in 1836 as Director of the Academy of Villa Medici and returned to Paris in 1841 when his artistic importance was finally acknowledged in his homeland.

Ingres had suffered so much during the rigid education he received from David that he himself in turn became strict, haughty and intolerant, with the result that his pupils tended to imitate him rather than try to understand him.

For Ingres, "lines" were all-important. A well-drawn picture was for him almost a painting. His model was Raphael and anyone who had different opinions about art was not worthy of his consideration.

So much for the negative side. On the positive side there is his extraordinary ability to construct distinct, harmonious drawings, similar in every way to those done by Italian painters during the Renaissance.

It is hardly surprising that such a determined quest for beauty made him unpopular with his contemporaries. Younger painters, however, like Degas and, later, Matisse, recognized him as a master and set out to follow his example.

*Jean-Auguste-Dominique Ingres
(1780-1867):* Study of Horse-Riders,
*1827-1834 – graphite, 54.4 × 41.3 cm –
Nelson Gallery – Atkins Museum,
Kansas City*

The Cartoon

The first thing we notice about this study is the care with which the model has been chosen. A painter must know how to choose his models according to the subject-matter he wishes to represent. In this case the ancient warrior is a man who uses the sword, carries a shield and probably wears a suit of armour. Throughout the war he has an enormous amount of weight to carry about.

He must therefore be as muscular as a heavyweight boxer. If the warrior carries a sword, the model could be a blacksmith or a peasant, since in their work both of them perform movements very similar to those of a warrior and their arm muscles will be similarly developed. The drawing is done with a stick of graphite of the type used before the invention of the pencil. The model has been drawn in several different positions in order to explore his aesthetic possibilities to the full before copying the final version onto the canvas.

The study, known in jargon as the cartoon, is copied onto the canvas in one of two ways, the first of which consists in dividing the chosen drawing up into little squares (as shown in the small figure in the lower right-hand corner). The horizontal and vertical lines making the squares are called coordinates.

Fix a piece of tracing paper over the drawing with adhesive tape (of the sort that will not tear the paper when it is removed). Draw the perimeter of the drawing on the tracing paper using an HB pencil and then divide the drawing up into little squares. Divide the canvas up into the same number of squares as the drawing, drawing the coordinates with a stick of charcoal or a charcoal pencil. Then copy the drawing onto the canvas, taking great care at the points where the figure intersects the coordinates. When the copying is finished, the drawing is ready to be coloured.

The second technique is known as pouncing and is used to transfer drawings made on special paper (pouncing paper) onto the canvas or other surface. The drawing must have exactly the same dimensions as the final painting. Holes are then made along the outline of the drawing and the pouncing paper is either fixed to the canvas with adhesive tape or pressed on using a special die impregnated with powdered carbon black or umber.

A dotted outline of the original drawing is thus left on the canvas. The technique is similar to the one used for copying designs onto cloth or for embroidery work.

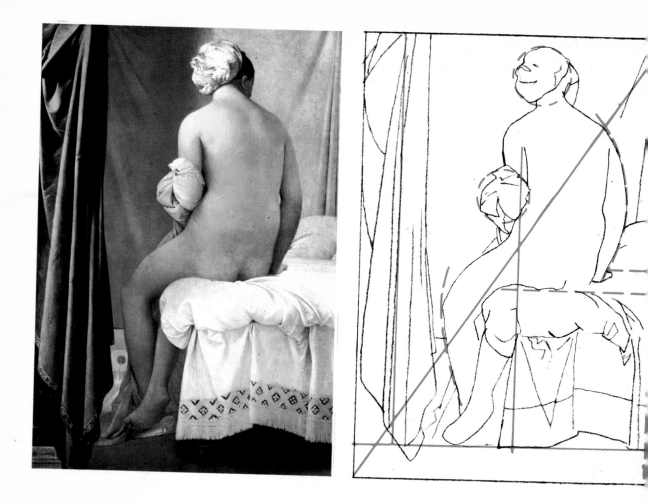

Ingres: *The Valpinçon Bather*

You must have seen reproductions of Ingres's *Bather* dozens of times. The painting of the young girl seen from the back is a work of great beauty and modernity.

But what is it that makes the painting so beautiful? Nowadays a woman with a body like this would hardly conform to popular standards of beauty. The modern ideal would be slimmer, with small breasts, far removed from the concept of woman as a child-bearer and mother, with a sturdy body made for bringing up children, chopping wood, doing the housework, milking the cows and helping her husband on the farm. A woman of this sort had little time for herself and, we might add, little time to worry about nervous breakdowns.

Jean-Auguste-Dominique Ingres:
The Valpinçon Bather, 1808 –
oil on canvas, 140 × 95 cm –
Louvre, Paris

This is why the body of the woman chosen by Ingres, though certainly not a peasant woman, conveys an extraordinary feeling of inner peace. The bed she is sitting on is white, soft and clean. You can almost smell the scent of Marseilles soap coming from the sheets.

Only one detail of the bed is highlighted: the elegant embroidery work around the edge. In those days girls spent years embroidering articles for their "bottom drawer". There is, however, another more important element in the painting which conveys a feeling of peace and serenity.

A few preliminary remarks are perhaps needed at this point.

If we draw a vertical line we create something visible joining the earth and the sky. It is something solid and secure like, for example, a cypress tree.

If, on the other hand, we draw a horizontal line, we create something which gives the impression of calm and continuity. If we add a cypress tree (a vertical line) to a landscape that stretches out towards the horizon (a horizontal line), we create a sensation of strength, order and peace.

What has all this got to do with the *Bather*? It provides the key to an understanding of the picture. If we look carefully, we will see that the green curtain on the left is the vertical line (the

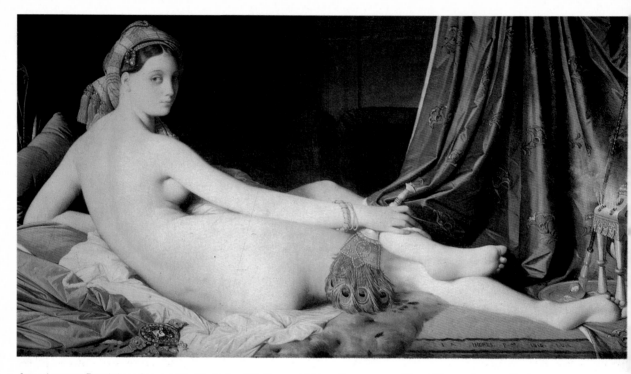

Jean-Auguste-Dominique Ingres: The Reclining Odalisque, *1814 – oil on canvas, 91 × 162 cm – Louvre, Paris*

"cypress tree"). The bed, with the white fore-ground and the horizon beneath the pillow, is the horizontal line.

The dark floor again gives a sense of the horizontal. This contrasts with the fold in the cloth in the background on the left. The fold continues on the sheet on the left-hand side of the bed. The figure seems to be closed in round brackets, the first being the left leg and the second the right arm. These two semi-curves also create a sense of peace and security, affording protection against outside forces. The right arm is vertical, on a perpendicular with the right leg. Horizontal contrast is provided by the line of the woman's body sitting on the bed. The whole picture is divided in two by a diagonal line running from the right shoulder to the point where the left leg touches the ground. Lastly, the turban on the woman's head and the sheet twisted round her arm create colour contrasts. We find them again a hundred years later in the paintings by Paul Klee. Having identified the rules of construction followed by Ingres in the *Bather*, we could begin to analyze the painting in even greater detail.

We must not forget, however, that the real aim of this book is to teach how to draw and paint the human figure.

Ingres: *The Reclining Odalisque*

Let us now analyze another painting by Ingres, *The Reclining Odalisque*. Again the harmony of the painting is the result of its geometrical structure. To speak of "geometry" and "structure" is to take nothing away from the painter's art. A painter with a "good hand" but with no sense of structure is like a ship with no one at the helm.

All good paintings are preceded by a series of preparatory sketches and studies. As the work proceeds the sketches are gradually included in the picture until each shape and each element of the picture is in harmony with those near it, thus creating the overall visual consonance of the final work.

We can begin our analysis of Ingres's *Odalisque* by examining the drapery. In the original sketch Ingres probably drew a rough shape of about the right size. Then, to draw the preparatory study or cartoon, he probably hung the cloth over a wooden frame, using nails to ensure that the folds were as he wanted them. The centre of the cloth in the picture is in fact perfectly vertical, with a semi-curve on either side. The curve on the left goes on to form a kind of overturned "S" with the feathers of the fan. The arms and the head form a triangle which cuts the parallelogram formed by the dark background perfectly in half. If we look carefully, we will find another triangle in the top left-hand corner and another beneath the woman's left leg. The curve of the backbone is the exact opposite of the curve formed by the cloth.

From all this we can see that painting is based on the calculated organization of instinct rather than on instinct alone.

Colour, for example, is also a part of the organization: it is essential to know your colours well and to learn how to use them perfectly. To do this, we must first take a close look at the artist's palette. It often happens that when the colours on the palette are properly organized the painting turns out to be well organized too. And vice versa. The first thing to learn, then, is the layout of the colours on the palette. Arrange the colours in the following order:

yellow ochre

pale cadmium yellow

deep cadmium yellow

vermilion red

carmine red

burnt sienna

burnt umber

Van Dyck brown

blue indigo

prussian blue

ultramarine blue

cerulean blue

turquoise

permanent green

emerald green

sap green

olive green

raw umber

titanium white

zinc white

The colour required must be found by mixing the colours on the palette and not, as sometimes happens, by looking through the tubes of paint to find one that looks more or less right. Remember that each colour must always contain a tiny percentage of its complementary colour. Every red must be softened with the slightest touch of green and every green with the slightest hint of red. Every yellow must contain a touch of violet and vice versa. The same goes for blues and oranges. If a colour has to be lightened, e.g. if you want to turn a blue into a light blue, always start with white and then add the blue gradually. If you start with blue, you will find that you will never get the exact shade required and you are likely to end up with an awful lot of paint on your palette. To darken a colour, always use the complement of the colour in question (never use black). Carmine red mixed with emerald green, for example, gives a result near to black; other "near blacks" can be obtained by mixing cadmium yellow with cobalt violet or ultramarine blue with cadmium orange. These blacks can be used to darken other colours. Try mixing the above colours to obtain the blacks and test their quality by adding some white; if the result is a neutral grey (i.e. neither too warm nor too cold), you can be sure that you have succeeded in obtaining the correct shade of black (the real name of which is "bistre"). If the grey is too warm, increase the amount of warm component; if it is too cold, increase the cold component.

It is also important to learn to see the world in terms of colours; for me, selecting the colours I would use to paint the objects or landscapes I see is something I do almost automatically. Obviously here we are speaking about tone painting where the colours are controlled; in other types of painting the colours can be used "pure", but this lies beyond the scope of this book.

Some of you may think that what I have said so far is somewhat cold and unemotional. This is because we are talking about a phase that comes after the emotion has been felt. Analysis serves to translate the inspiration into a picture which will convey the emotional feeling to the observer. We all have feelings but not everyone knows how to express them. This extract from an essay by Delacroix may help us to understand this point better.

"We have to take from the model only what we need to express our idea. The form of the model, whether it be a tree or a man, is merely the dictionary the artist uses to confirm his own impressions and help him remember them. Planning a composition means combining known elements with others that belong to the artist's inner soul. Many artists, though, compose with the model in front of them; maybe they take away some things and add others, but their starting point is always an extraneous object, the exterior model. They are therefore dominated by the influence of nature as it is and this explains why in some of these paintings we are aware of an amazing sterility and lack of warmth. If these artists then decide to add some extra details, they still insist on making an exact imitation of whatever it was that so weakly inspired them. A model is, of course, necessary and indeed essential, but it must be a slave to the artist's creative talents. The model provides the artist with certain details that even the liveliest imagination and the most accurate memory could never reproduce and at the same time it confirms and consecrates what the imagination has produced. Needless to say, great skill is required for this task and it may take a lifetime to acquire it. When I say that only certain details of the model are used, this must not be taken as imposing absolute limits; every system has its own rules as to how much imitation is admitted. Holbein and Memling are sublime not in spite of their extraordinary ability to imitate but because of it. It all depends on the spirit in which the imitation is made."

Delacroix's words are full of useful hints and suggestions.

The painter must be able to find ideas and inspiration in any figure. A fat woman can create as much figurative interest as one with a perfect body. Nature makes no mistakes when it creates people as they are.

The shape of the human figure changes according to the position it is in; every new pose thus transforms the expressive possibilities of the body. The shapes we know and remember best are usually those of the people nearest to us. It is very likely that Ingres saw the pose he used for his *Bather* in the woman he loved, perhaps many years before he actually painted the painting. Perhaps he saw the woman in that position for a brief moment only, and yet certain details remained impressed on his mind: the crossed legs and the slope of the back, for example. The most important thing is that it aroused feelings in him that he never forgot. Later, Ingres must have looked for a model with the same physical features. He added the elements we have analyzed as well as his skill and his inimitable technique: his ability to mix colours and to match or contrast them, and his knowledge of how to prepare his canvas, something which is just as important as knowing how to observe and how to draw. A badly prepared canvas spoils the painting before it has even been started. A painter must learn to love his models and he must also love the ritual of getting ready to paint.

Let us now take a look at how to prepare a canvas and how to fix it to the frame.

Preparing Canvases, Panels and Boards

There are many ways of preparing the support; here I will simply describe two of the easiest methods.

First method

Leave four handfuls of rabbit glue to soak in half a litre of cold water for twelve hours (do this the

33

night before). The granules will swell up but they should remain separate. If they stick together when cold it means that the glue is of poor quality and must be changed. After twelve hours, bring a pan of water to the boil and put the tin containing the glue into it. Boil the tin gently until the glue dissolves.

To check whether the glue is ready for use, take some of the liquid between your thumb and index finger and press your fingers together to feel the stickiness. If it is too sticky, add a little hot water; if it is not sticky enough repeat the whole operation from the beginning increasing the amount of glue. It follows that it is best to use plenty of glue from the start.

Mix together equal amounts of Bologna plaster and kaolin plaster; add the equivalent amount of glue to the plaster mixture (1:1) as well as a 1/2 part of boiled linseed oil. Mix well and then spread the mixture onto the canvas or board with a flat, wide- bristle brush. The mixture cannot be kept: it will go hard when cool and will start to go bad after 24 hours.

Second method

For a mixture that is less white than the previous one, use two parts of Bologna plaster and one of grey clay (this is the type of clay used by sculptors and is on sale in paint shops; it must be dried and then crushed). Add water to obtain a semi-liquid paste with no lumps; then mix with an equal quantity of lukewarm rabbit glue (prepared as described in the previous method). If the glue and paste fail to mix well, put the tin containing the mixture into a pan of boiling water and boil gently until a good mixture is obtained. If the paste is not sticky enough, add more glue. To make the mixture smoother, add boiled linseed oil in the proportion of 1:10.

How to Fix the Canvas on the Frame

The most commonly used canvases are made of coarse linen (unbleached), hemp or cotton. Canvases made of synthetic fibres are not suitable for oil painting.

Before putting the canvas onto the frame it must be soaked in water.

The frame may be square, rectangular, round or oval; it is also possible to have special shapes made by a good carpenter.

Rectangular frames are the most common; these consist of four strips of wood which fit together at the ends by means of tenon and mortise joints.

Frames larger than one metre normally have a fifth strip of wood running diagonally across the frame to prevent torsion when the canvas dries. Good quality frames have two wedges at each of the four corners to hold the canvas firm when the painting has been completed. The wedges must be tapped gently with a hammer until the canvas is held taut.

The Model's Pose

An artist can find inspiration in anything at all. Nevertheless he is bound to be inspired most by the things he loves.

Leonardo da Vinci said that when you love something you want to get to know it really well in order to love it even more. It is not easy to draw or paint a nude human figure and make it beautiful rather than vulgar. Every position of the body or face conveys a certain message.

Imagine, for example, a female nude with the same physical features in three different positions: the first with both hands modestly covering her sex and with no movement of the body; the second with the body leaning slightly to one side, with one arm covering the breasts and the other hand covering the sex, and the third with one hand covering the sex and the other over the mouth.

The three figures convey three entirely different messages: the first represents a female martyr, the second is a Venus figure, while the third

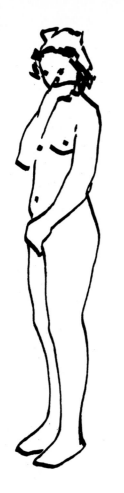

could have come straight out of a nineteenth century book of humorous cartoons. The three different messages are conveyed by the pose of the model.

It is therefore always a good idea to make small-scale studies before starting the larger work. Before copying a model in the studio, draw a series of rough sketches of the poses he or she is to adopt, carefully following the bone structure.

Another series of preparatory studies can be made by copying people sitting or lying on the beach or on the banks of rivers. This kind of subject-matter has been used in the past by many great artists. Cézanne, for example, worked for years on the *Great Bathers*, perhaps his most important work.

The small studies and the watercolour shown on the next pages are excellent examples of what we are saying about the importance of small sketches. The greatness of Cézanne never ceases to astound me.

Three examples of female nudes in different poses

Paul Cézanne (1839-1906): Studies for Bathers, *1873-1877 – pencil and pen on thin paper, 20 × 30.1 cm –*
Kupferstichkabinett der Öffentlichen Kunstsammlung, Basel

Cézanne's Watercolour

Looking carefully at Cézanne's watercolour, we see how the pencil-drawn outline, which for Ingres had to be geometrically perfect, becomes a way of animating the figures. The sketchy double lines create an effect that is similar to that of a slightly blurred photograph.

The line appears to change as if by metamorphosis from a static outline into a vibrant movement in which the area surrounding the figure blends and intermingles with the area inside the figure. The colour is applied using the same vibrant movement.

Cézanne used this technique to transform the optical effect of perspective, which until then was

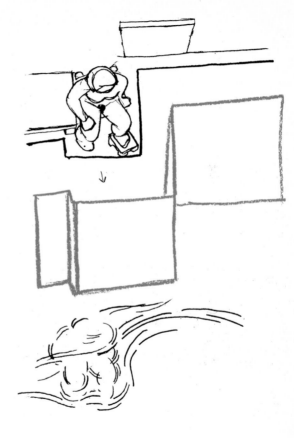

1

2

essential in order to achieve a three-dimensional result, into a vibrant effect of interpenetrating lines and colours. Imagine we are looking at a painting drawn using traditional perspective at right angles from above; the result is similar to the example shown in "1".

If we do the same with a painting by Cézanne, on the other hand, the result is like example "2".

Like all great painters, Cézanne was a perfectionist. A painter who concentrates more on quantity than on quality cannot be taken seriously from a professional point of view. Cézanne required the model to sit for him 150 times to paint a figure. Assuming that each sitting lasted three hours, he worked for a total of 450 hours. Cézanne created a second revolution in the world of painting by reducing the various techniques to one. In other words, when Cézanne painted in oils he obtained the same effects as he did with watercolours and

On the left: Paul Cézanne (1839-1906): Standing Nude, *ca. 1895 – pencil and watercolour sketch, 89 × 53 cm – Louvre, Paris*

On the right: Paul Cézanne: The Great Bathers, *1898-1905 – oil on canvas, 208 × 249 cm – Philadelphia Museum of Art, Wilstach Collection*

Pablo Picasso (1881-1973): Study for Les Demoiselles d'Avignon – *page of a sketchbook – Paris, Spring 1907 – pencil, 19.5 × 24.2 cm – Picasso Museum, Paris*

when he painted in watercolours he obtained the same vibrations that can be achieved when working with pencil. And it was precisely with watercolours that he introduced the most important innovations.

The art of watercolour, a genre which at that time was considered most suitable for young ladies, had been transformed by Constable into a violent, sensual form of painting, though it had lost none of its basic delicacy and transparency. Cézanne took the process even further and made watercolour as important as Renaissance painting. He

42

had a wonderful control over colour, achieved by working on several parts of the painting at the same time so that the colours of one part could be drying while he worked on another part. When the colours were dry he went over them again making them warmer or colder, and so on until the painting was completed. The result is a very special sensation of spaces filled with light breezes of coloured air which combine to form a landscape, a still life or a nude. Many twentieth-century artists, especially those who devoted themselves to abstract painting, have tried to emulate this technique, but the quality of the effect achieved by Cézanne has never been matched.

For Cézanne, painting was as natural as breathing. He would spend weeks or even months painting a still life and was never fully satisfied with the final result. In this sense we can say that Cézanne was like a farmer who ploughed the land, sowed the seed and looked after the plants but never saw the harvest. The "fruit" was picked in later years by Picasso, Braque, the Cubists, Futurists and abstract painters in general.

Modern painters should try to forget everything they have seen or felt and return to the teachings of Cézanne.

Painting Figures

Let's now set about learning how to paint the human figure.

First of all you have to learn to see with other eyes, ridding yourself of any preconceived ideas. You have to learn to know yourself so that you know and understand others and are able to copy them.

Never trust any latter-day "Bohemians" who paint under the influence of alcohol or drugs; their work never looks like anything else than the work of drunkards or drug-addicts. It is true that there are plenty of stories about painters who have been ruined by absinthe or the like; if we read their biographies carefully, however, we realize that they had suffered so much humiliation during their lives that they turned to alcohol not as a source of inspiration but as a desperate means of escape.

One of the first things to learn is to how to observe the natural positions of the human figure in everyday life.

Have you ever noticed how much dignity is expressed by a female figure sitting in the position shown in the drawing? Very little power of observation is needed to realize that a person sitting in this position reveals hardly any inner emotion and has a great deal of almost regal pride and self-respect. She probably walks with short, quick steps, without moving her body too much. Even if we take her clothes off in this position, she will keep her dignity intact.

And now, to work. Sit your model in the position required. Remember that the chair and other objects which will be part of the painting are extremely important. Never rush when preparing things that are to be copied or painted. If you can, go and see a good fashion or advertising photographer at work: he will spend hours arranging all the various articles, checking constantly to ensure that his lens captures the correct frame. A painter has the advantage of being able to sketch his picture before making the final version. If you

want to copy your model in one position only, you can get her to sit on a chair, a sofa or a deck-chair. If you are doing a more detailed study and require her to sit in various positions, get her to sit on a stool.

Draw your sketch on a sheet of paper measuring 70 x 100 cm, fixing the paper to a piece of laminboard the same size with thumbtacks. It is best not to use a plywood board for various reasons: the tacks will come loose too easily, the surface is never perfectly smooth and plywood is too heavy. The job of fixing the paper to the board is more difficult than it may seem. I have often seen art students drawing on paper that has been badly fixed to their boards and the results are often disastrous. Set your board flat on a table and then tack down the upper corners of the paper first. Use your hands to smooth down the paper until all the air bubbles have been eliminated, starting from the right-hand side. Now tack down the lower right-hand corner. Continue smoothing and tacking, finishing with the lower left-hand corner. If the paper is very large, add extra tacks, halfway between the others. The support to which you attach your paper should extend at least two inches beyond the paper. To avoid problems, be ready with supports of different sizes.

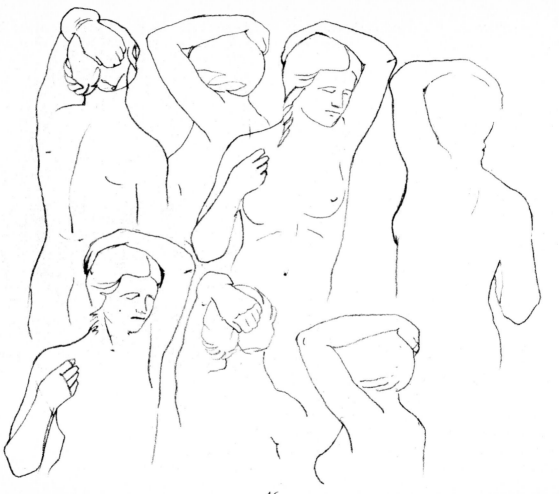

Let's go back now to the working position. Stand in front of the easel with the paper positioned vertically.

Start by doing a rough sketch of the head, which serves as the unit of measurement and also to check that the drawing is correctly centered. From the head, draw lines following the inclination of the body, using a plumb-line if necessary. A plumb-line is a tool used by builders for determining perpendicularity. It is held between the thumb and the index finger as shown in the example on page 65, and helps to make the sketch geometrically balanced.

One of the techniques used by painters to sketch nudes consists of the use of charcoal.

Nude Studies in Charcoal

Charcoal is the technique normally used by painters to make preparatory sketches for oil paintings, tempera paintings and watercolours. If we look at the example of rotation in the drawings, we can see how the extension of the coordinates of the first drawing serves as a point of reference for the second. The second drawing has been sketched but not shaded in, while the third is an outline showing the methods used.

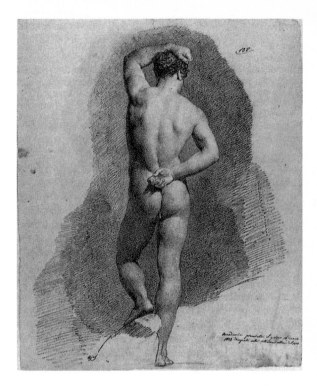

Francesco Hayez (1791-1882):
Study of a Male Nude, *1812 –*
Archiginnasio – Palagi Collection
Bologna

47

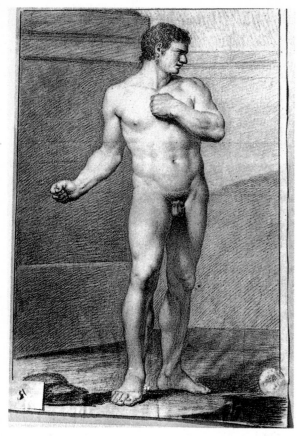

Francesco Hayez: Study of a Male Nude – *charcoal,*
58.5 × 38.5 cm – Accademia di Belle Arti, Venice

Male Nudes by Francesco Hayez

Francesco Hayez was Italy's answer to Ingres. In my opinion there are many similarities between the two painters, though not all critics would agree with me on this point.

At the beginning of this century Carlo Carrà wrote that Hayez was "the only Italian painter able to match the extraordinary success that Ingres had had with the French Neopurists," adding that "Hayez is not understood despite the fact that this is called the period of 'pure painting'."

Both Ingres and Hayez studied in Rome during the same period and were influenced by Raphael. The plasticity and harmony of the muscles in these two drawings bear witness to the severity and precision of the teaching the artist had received. The frontal nude, in fact, won Hayez first prize in a competition organized by the Venice Academy. Within the Academy at that time there was much controversy about how the painting of the nude should be taught.

Pietro Edwards, who was elected President of the Academy in 1793, had this to say about the situation he found:

"There was no teacher of anatomy to give basic instruction in this subject and then apply the principles to living nude specimens.

No one taught the students how to select beautiful human forms and neither were they able to consult anatomical charts or plaster statues with the muscles marked on them.

No famous statues were ever placed near the nude model so that the young students could see how nature should be imitated and thus learn to avoid mistakes.

The model was never made to adopt poses made famous by ancient statues."

Study in the Academies alternated with the observation of classical statues. When Hayez made his sketch of Carolina Zucchi in bed, he followed the method he had learnt in the Academy, where, as a young student, he had practised by making copies of a rotating plaster statue of a male torso.

Copies of a Plaster Statue of a Male Torso Drawn by My Students

Many of you will find it very difficult to copy models because, for obvious reasons, a model is never completely still.

Beginners will also tend to concentrate on details, especially the face, thus losing sight of the whole. The important thing is not to lose heart. Go out and buy some plaster copies of classical statues. They are not easy to find but are available from specialized art shops or modellers (you can get a list of these by asking at your local art school).

If you wish to know the human figure in even greater detail, you might even try to get hold of one of the plaster casts made of human bodies used by medical students in anatomy lessons. Copying and interpreting such casts is an extremely useful exercise for would-be artists.

I am now going to show you two studies drawn by my own students.

The first was done by Luisella Lissoni on pouncing paper (see on page 50). After making a rough sketch of the figure, she proceeded to sketch the face as a guide to the rest.

Naturally the paper is held firmly in place by thumbtacks. Shading is done by means of cross-hatching, without making too much of a contrast between the dark shades, half-tones and the lighter areas. If cartridge paper is used, you can achieve highlighting effects by using white chalk or ceruse.

In the drawing in question, Luisella has also shaded the wall against which the plaster torso rests in order to create more volume and make the effect more dramatic.

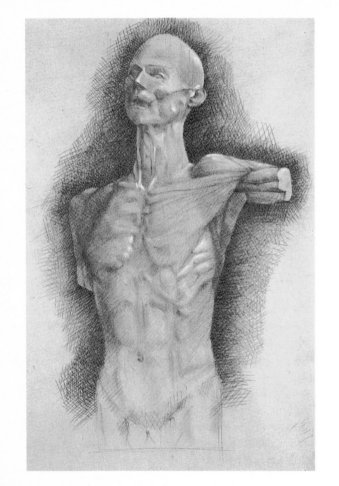

The Torso Drawn by Gianfranco Pugni

The paper chosen by this student was the slightly rough paper normally used for watercolours. Much care has been taken over the drawing and it is clear that Gianfranco has tried to give the plaster torso vitality and vibrance.

Like Luisella, Gianfranco started with a lightly drawn outline of the head and then the rest of the body.

Making an anatomical drawing expressive is obviously a step towards expressionism. Gianfranco has drawn only the torso and has not attempted to give it any particular environment. The result is a drawing of great delicacy. Again we see how a good drawing is often the same as a good painting: the two can never be separated.

If you have difficulty finding plaster statues, my advice is to start by copying very thin models. It was this type of figure that most inspired the expressionist painters and some of their works are practically anatomical studies. The work of Egon Schiele is a case in point.

On the left: Luisella Lissoni: Copy of a Plaster Statue – *pencil and white pastel on pouncing paper*

On the right: Gianfranco Pugni: Copy of a Plaster Statue – *pencil on pouncing paper*

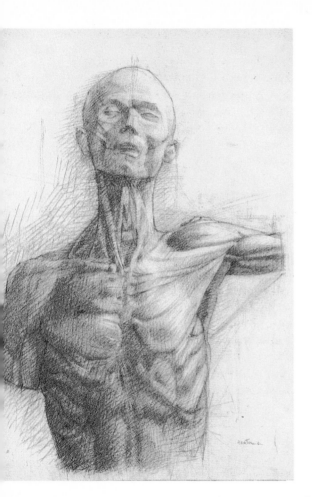

Egon Schiele: *Female Nude*

Egon Schiele was born on June 12, 1890 at Tulln, a small town on the Danube about 40 miles from Vienna. The sixth child of Adolf Eugen Schiele, a railway clerk, and Marie Soukup, of Bohemian origin, Egon got good marks at school only in art. In 1905 his father died of the after-effects of a venereal disease. Shocked by this death, Egon was later to give expression to his inner drama in his drawings. In 1906 he studied with Strauch, academically painting still life studies, landscapes and religious subjects. Against the wishes of his uncle and guardian, his mother helped him to enter the Academy of Figurative Arts (Akademie der bildenden Künste) of Vienna.

From 1908 onwards he was definitely in contact with Klimt. In November 1911 he became a member of the "Sema" group in Munich, to which Klee and Kufin also belonged.

On April 13, 1913 he was arrested on charges of immorality and the corruption of minors. He spent twenty-four days in prison before being acquitted of the most serious of the charges. In 1913 he became part of the Bund Österreichischer Kunstler (League of Austrian Artists) whose President was Klimt. When Klimt died in 1918, Schiele became the most representative exponent of artistic life in the Austrian capital. In the autumn of the same year, however, he fell victim to the outbreak of Spanish fever that was raging in Vienna at the time and died on October 31, just a few hours before the announcement of the end of the First World War.

Schiele grew up artistically in the Vienna of Freud, Weininger, Kraus and Musil. He was fascinated by Van Gogh, Ensor, Munch and Klimt. He had love affairs with many of his models, the most famous of whom was Wally Neuzil who was his companion for many years. His nudes reflect the soul of a corrupt society and often seem like dead bodies in an advanced state of decay. It is the same kind of decay as that which Schiele saw in the society around him. Critics were hostile to him, however, and his greatest works were considered pornographic and immoral.

If we look at the technique used in this painting, we see the importance Schiele attached to the line used to construct the figure. He is basically saying what Ingres had said before him: a well-drawn picture is in itself a painting, or, in other words, a painting is no more than a coloured drawing. Looking more closely, we see that the figure has been drawn quickly and if the artist has second thoughts he makes corrections without rubbing out what he had originally drawn, resulting in a somewhat contorted effect. The artist's sensibility thus "harmonically deforms" the original drawing. The figure therefore no longer has classical lines but gains in expressivity.

In all probability the drawing was done in charcoal and then preserved with fixative. The colour is a tempera quite unlike anything on the market today. It is probably a casein tempera applied with a flat bristle brush. We can try to reproduce it by mixing powder pigment with casein glue. Casein glue is obtained in the following way: take some dry casein (available in good art shops and paint shops) and let 10 grams of the powder soak in 50 grams of cold water for 20 minutes, stirring well with a stick (do not use a metal implement since this could spoil the glue) until it dissolves. Then slowly add 2 grams of ammonia until the solution is dense. Continue stirring and add 5 grams of glycerine.

Filter the mixture through a muslin cloth or a nylon stocking to obtain the glue. This type of glue will keep for only 24 hours; after this time it will start to go off and has to be thrown away. Also remember that, once dried, the glue cannot be regenerated and so it is essential to wash the brush well after use.

Mix the powder paint with water and add glue using a brush. Keep it dense if you want an effect

ike that of the hair in the painting, or dilute with
water to make it thinner, as Schiele did when
painting the body. The bluish, greenish glaze can
be achieved by means of the so-called "dry glaze"
technique.
Let us try out this technique ourselves. To paint
with the "dry glaze" technique, use a flat, hard
bristle brush (synthetic brushes are not at all suitable for this type of painting), keeping a piece of
paper handy (an old newspaper will do).
Dilute the powder paint with water until it has the
density of olive oil, take some on the tip of the
brush and rub it on the newspaper (using the brush
movement normally used by house- painters to
paint the walls of a room) until the mark left by
the brush is similar to a scratch.
Now pass the brush gently over your painting to
create the glaze effect. Take some powder paints
(even inexpensive ones will do) and some casein
glue. Since the glue is quite difficult to prepare,
my advice is to use an industrial product such as
wallpaper paste or vinavil. When vinavil dries, it

gon Schiele (1890-1918): Female Nude – 44.3 × 30.6 cm –
raphische Sammlung Albertina, Vienna

is almost transparent; when fresh, however, it is milky in colour and tends to lighten the powder paints.

Another problem is the fact that when powder paints are wet they become darker and then return to their original colour when they dry. It is therefore best to mix up the dry powders first until the required shade of colour is obtained and then add the water and the glue. This method works with any kind of glue.

After examining Schiele's painting, I drew a study of a female figure. My aim was to try to understand the technique used by the great artist. I drew the outline in charcoal, making the model look thinner than she really was. Then I mixed my powder paints: titanium white with yellow ochre and a little vermilion, adding some ultramarine blue to the first mixture. By toning up or down the warm colours, like red and yellow, and the cold

Nude drawn following the style of Schiele

colours, like green and blue, I tried to reproduce the dramatic effect of Schiele's nude. The violet shades are obtained by adding a touch of carmine and ultramarine to the flesh colour. When mixing the colours together on the palette, remember to start from the dominant colour, adding small amounts of the colour used to vary the shade. For example, to get dark green, you start with ultramarine blue and then gradually add pale cadmium yellow until achieving the exact shade required.

If it is still not quite right, you can adjust it with permanent green, Verona green or terre verte from a tube. The important thing is not to paint with the colours straight from the tube. Light green is obtained by starting with pale cadmium yellow and gradually adding ultramarine until the shade of green is right. It is best never to use lemon yellow when trying to make green.

Let's get back to my female figure. The reddish part of the stomach and the right thigh was obtained by adding a touch of carmine to the basic flesh colour. Blue on the eyelids and black for the hair. It is best to get the black by mixing carmine, ultramarine and pale cadmium yellow or by mixing Van Dyck brown with ultramarine. The colour thus obtained is called bistre and is used instead of black to darken other colours.

It can also be mixed with white to make grey. The colours obtained by adding bistre are completely different from those we get if we add black. If we darken yellow with black we get a greenish shade without any real character of its own. If we use bistre, on the other hand, the yellow will have a very particular kind of gloss.

Now you try to interpret the human figure as an expressionist would have done. Choose the painter you like the most and find out as much as you can about him: how he lived, his favourite authors, his friends and the type of model he used.

Try to live as he did (within reasonable limits, of course) until you begin to see with his eyes, to use his colours and follow his lines. Obviously every painter must have his own personality, but you will find that studying a great artist in this way will be of great artistic value to you. When I began to study Cézanne in depth I discovered that he repeated the same subject over and over again, continuously varying the viewpoint and the effects of the light. What was he searching for?

Once the painting had been completed from the point of view of perspective and the optical effect of the third dimension (a painter works in two dimensions, width and height: depth is obtained through the optical effect), it was necessary to create the sensation of time. If we look at one of Michelangelo's unfinished works, we get a definite sensation of time. The sculptures seem to leave a message saying that they are waiting for the artist to come back and finish his work. A pencil sketch on a piece of paper gives the same impression. Cézanne's pictures also give this sensation of something unfinished and thus create the feeling of time.

Puberty, by Edvard Munch

Egon Schiele died at the age of 28. Edvard Munch was born at Löten twenty-seven years before the birth of Schiele. Schiele's paintings expressed morbid sexuality; Munch's expressed physical and moral suffering. He succeeded in conveying the anguish of his tormented state of mind.

Munch's childhood was marked by the deaths of his mother and his sister, and these tragic events had a predominating influence on his literary tastes and his painting.

A great friend of Strindberg and an avid reader of the works of Kirkegaard, he struggled throughout his life against middle-class prejudice and conventional moralism. He was physically strong and lived to the age of 80, despite his constant desire for death which, in 1908, led to his being admitted to the hospital run by Dr. Jacobsen in Copenhagen. When he came out of hospital he was cured, but after that date his paintings were never the same again.

Munch was greatly influenced by the Impressionists: Van Gogh, Toulouse-Lautrec and, above all, Gauguin. For Van Gogh, real women were those who shared the hardship and suffering of their male companions; for Toulouse-Lautrec, they were the women of the Moulin Rouge; and for Gauguin, they were the primitive women of the South Seas. For Munch, the image of a woman was the image of a sick body and his female nudes are often obsessive for this very reason.

It is not easy to express feelings of this sort through painting. To transform colours which to most people's eyes are vivid and bright into livid, leaden hues implies toning down all the colours on the palette.

We can experiment with this by performing the following exercise. Choose a fragile-looking model with the body of an adolescent. Draw her sitting up straight, in profile.

A nude painted in ordinary colours has a pinkish colour obtained by mixing yellow ochre with light vermilion and zinc white. The light part of her

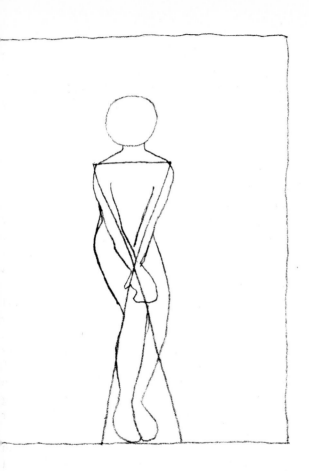

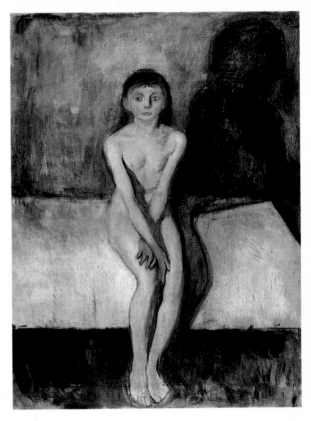

Edvard Munch (1863-1944): Puberty, *1893 – oil on canvas. 149 × 112 cm – Munch Museum, Oslo*

stockings is vermilion and the dark part vermilion plus carmine. Now paint the same figure again, mixing 10% of raw umber to the colours previously used. The result is a figure with an aura of sadness about her. If you add terre verte instead of raw umber, the figure begins to look like a corpse. If you add cobalt violet, the result is a kind of ghost.

After doing the above exercise, take a close look at Munch's painting. Its basic structure is the triangle.

The colour of the girl's body has shades of blue and violet. The shadow on the wall is creeping up behind like death and there is an expression of infinite sadness on the girl's face. Puberty here is seen as a reason for deep gloom and depression.

Boy Pulling a Rope, by Pellizza da Volpedo

Nowadays art schools are attended by young people from all social classes and origins. If we look back to the 1950s and 1960s, however, the situation was rather different. In those days it was important to find a "real" job and to start earning as soon as possible. Going even further back in time, imagine how difficult things must have been for young men wishing to make a career out of painting at the start of the nineteenth century in Italy. When, for example, Pellizza da Volpedo wanted to enter the Academy of Brera, he had to struggle against prejudices arising from his social origins and his position as an active socialist. He was the son of a farm labourer and devoted himself to painting with the determination and strength his father used to till the land: method, constancy and love for a career which rewarded him very little during his brief lifetime. Art critics have also treated him harshly, often relegating him to the position of a minor artist.

The drawings we are going to look at, two studies of a young boy pulling a rope, were done in charcoal and pencil on beige paper and show clearly the teachings of Tallone in Bergamo, under whom Pellizza studied.

The skill of the artist lies in the repetition of slender strokes used for the outline which manage to give the impression of movement. The second

Opposite: Giuseppe Pellizza da Volpedo (1868- 1907): Boy Pulling a Rope – charcoal on paper, 40.6 × 30.7 cm; right: Study of a Nude – Bonomelli Collection, Milan

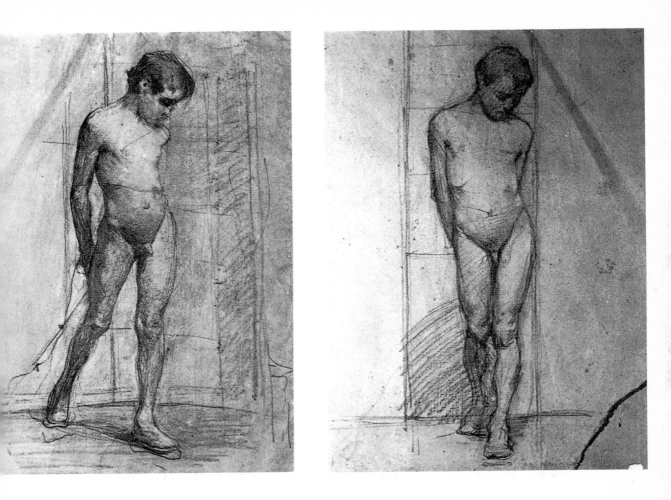

of the two drawings shows the same figure seen from the front. The method is quite clear: a series of points making up a triangular structure which serves as the basis for the whole drawing.

In Pellizza's words: "To draw a nude you have to find the three basic points forming the triangle which contains almost the whole figure and then worry about the horizontal lines, the spaces which serve to show that all the parts of the drawing are correct; you must never exaggerate anything when copying the nude since exaggeration leads to mistakes; the more exact the copy, the better the drawing is."

Woman Pulling up Her Stocking, by Henri de Toulouse-Lautrec

Vincent van Gogh said that "people are the reason for everything" and yet his sources of inspiration were chiefly landscapes and nature, just like all the impressionists. Toulouse-Lautrec was the only one who painted only the human figure, and his work became the only thing that gave sense to his short life. He died of alcoholism at the age of thirty-seven.

Born into a noble French family, whose ancestry went back to Charlemagne, he was a sickly child from birth. Two riding accidents in his youth left him deformed for the rest of his life. Born on November 24, 1864, he was a Sagittarius and therefore apparently superficial, cheerful, always ready to joke and even to laugh at his own deformity; in reality, however, his was an embittered, rigorously severe personality, with keen powers of observation. He got on badly with his father, but was greatly loved by his mother in whose arms he died.

In 1878 Toulouse-Lautrec met the Venetian painter Federico Zandomeneghi. From him he learned how to choose unusual visual angles, how to organize his subject matter and how to make his characters move beyond the improvised square of the canvas.

Though his pictures give the impression of having been painted quickly, they are in fact the result of painstakingly methodical work. His models would be made to pose for session after session.

Maurice Joyant reported that he had to sit for seventy-five sessions before Toulouse-Lautrec was finally satisfied with his portrait. He used to study his models at length, taking in forms and volumes. He used to concentrate on the models like a sprinter getting ready for the hundred metres and would then "throw himself" into the painting until all his energy had been used up. He often spent longer over the drawing than over the painting itself.

It is also worth remembering that Toulouse-Lautrec was another artist who believed in the teachings of Ingres regarding the basic importance of the line.

Toulouse-Lautrec's women are of two types: the first have gentle faces, bringing to mind the portrait of Toulouse-Lautrec's own mother, with their eyes gazing into the distance searching for happiness, submissive to destiny rather than protagonists; the others are the dubious characters from the brothels, the bistros and the Moulin Rouge, caught in their intimacy as if the artist was looking at them through the keyhole. Toulouse-Lautrec transformed these lost, scandalous women into the artistic masterpieces exhibited in major art galleries all over the world.

Henri de Toulouse-Lautrec (1864-1901):
Woman Pulling up Her Stocking –
oil on cardboard, 61.5 × 44.5 cm –
Toulouse-Lautrec Museum, Albi

Let's now take a look at Toulouse-Lautrec's painting of a woman pulling up her stockings. The painting is done on rough cardboard, raw umber in colour. It is a cheap, delicate kind of cardboard which soon loses its shape if exposed to humidity. The figure has been skilfully drawn using a brush. The background colour varies between bistre, pure burnt sienna and burnt sienna mixed with a touch of white. The flesh-coloured outline of the figure is a mixture of zinc white, yellow ochre and a hint of vermilion. The outline is cross-hatched like a pastel drawing, using a bristle brush (probably one with a filbert tip); only the parts in the light are coloured in since the colour of the board itself is used for the rest of the body. For the colour of the face some carmine has been added to the original colour prepared, with touches of ultramarine blue for the more shaded areas. The garment round the woman's neck is cerulean blue mixed with turquoise; her hair is a mixture of cadmium yellow and vermilion, and her stockings are prussian blue with a touch of burnt umber. The colours are all diluted with oil of turpentine so that they have the texture of watercolours. Although sketches and pencilled outlines are normally thought of as unfinished works, this particular painting by Toulouse-Lautrec, however hastily drawn, is not to be thought of in that way. It is the artist who decides when his painting is finished. If the highest expression of the subject-matter can be achieved after just a few strokes of the brush, the result would be spoiled by continuing any further. The important thing is to know exactly when to stop and learning to do this often implies making courageous decisions.

Odalisque au Tambourin, by Henri Matisse

Henri Matisse was born at Cateau-Cambrésis in Northern France on December 31, 1869. He studied law in Paris and then returned to his home town to take up employment as a bailiff. Until he was twenty-one he had never heard of Impressionism and had never even been inside an art exhibition or a picture gallery. Then, when he was convalescing after a long illness, his mother gave him a box of paints to help him pass the time. It was then that he found his real vocation. He attended a few art classes and then in 1891, against his father's will, he left for Paris to study at the Académie Julian. In 1892 he attended evening classes at the School of Decorative Arts and became friendly with Marquet. By 1895 he was studying with Rouault, Desvallières, Piot, Manguin and others in the studio of Gustave Moreau

Henri Matisse (1869-1954):
Odalisque au Tambourin, 1926 –
Oil on canvas, 73 × 54 cm –
Private Collection, New York

In 1896 and 1897 John Russel introduced him to Rodin and Pissarro. In 1898 he studied the human figure in an Academy on Rue de Rennes, where he met Dérain and Jean Puy and, encouraged by Rodin, began to take an interest in sculpture. From 1901 onwards his works were exhibited regularly at the Salon des Indépendants and the first exhibition of his own works was held in 1904 at the Vollard Gallery. In the same year Matisse followed Signac to St. Tropez and experimented with pointillism. In 1906 he met Picasso and in the following years travelled widely in Europe. By 1911 he had opened his own Academy and until 1917 he lived at Issy-les-Moulineaux, where he painted some of his greatest works for the Russian collectors Shukin and Morosov. From 1917 to his death in 1954 he travelled around the world. He died on November 3, 1954 in the hills near Ciniez, amidst the countryside he had loved so much.

Matisse was Picasso's great rival. He tended to simplify rather than innovate. Initially concerned chiefly with tonality, he later burst out in an explosion of colour. In terms of structure and sheer energy, he followed the examples set by Cézanne. In Matisse's paintings colours are dynamic forces which the artist tries to balance and control. With the rise of Cubism and the disintegration of the Fauvist movement, Matisse was left to explore hi chosen path alone.

Many of the artists who paved the way for moder painting were stimulated in their efforts by thei own existential problems. For painters like Va Gogh, Cézanne, Gauguin and, going back in time Michelangelo and Caravaggio, art was the ver reason for their existence. This was not the cas with Matisse. He innovated through the use o logic. "The painter's compass," he would hav said, "is the plumb line."

If you hold a plumb line with your arm stretche straight out in front of you, and look at you subject with one eye closed, you can find all th connecting points along the vertical line forme by the plumb line. You can do the same with horizontal line by holding your pencil perfectl flat in front of you while looking at your subjec with one eye closed. You will then be able to se all the points along that horizontal line. As yo begin to discover the structure of your subject b following its coordinates, note them on you paper. This will give you the characteristic con struction lines that are often found in the works o old masters.

By using these construction lines, you will draw what is basically a geometrical sketch. It is a error to reject this way of drawing "a priori,

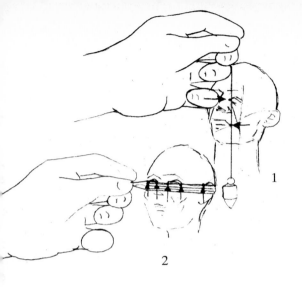

1

2

the scandal his paintings caused during the Fauvist Exhibition.

The fact is that his paintings heightened beauty

ince it is the only way to learn how to draw udes. All artists specializing in the human figure nd nudes learned gradually by using similar techiques.

Look carefully at this drawing and try to understand the function of each line: some mark the idden bone structure while others show the vertical and horizontal coordinates.

Never rub out the construction lines; they give olidity to the drawing. If you examine drawings one by old masters you will always find traces of he construction lines.

But let's go back to Matisse. He was amazed by

rather than merely depicting reality. With regard to colour, Matisse had this to say: "The predominant tendency of colour must be to help the artist express his feelings. I use my colours without any preconceived ideas if at first glance, and perhaps without my even being aware of it, a certain colour has captivated me; more often than not, it is not until after I have completed the painting that I realize that I have respected that colour by progressively modifying and transforming all the others. I am instinctively drawn towards the expressive side of colours. My choice of colours is not based on any scientific theory; it is based upon observation, feeling and the experience of my sensitivity. Taking inspiration from certain passages written by Delacroix, an artist such as Signac becomes concerned about complementary colours and his theoretical knowledge of them induces him to use one or another.

As for me, I merely try to use colors that express a certain feeling. There is a necessary balance in colours which enables them to modify the shape of the figure or which completely transforms my composition. I strive to achieve this balance and go on working until I have achieved it in every part of my painting.

Then comes the moment when I have achieved overall balance between all the parts and when it would be impossible for me to make even the slightest adjustment without having to retouch the whole painting."

These remarks show the firm logic with which Matisse approached his art. Instinctively he seems to seek out fixed points such as the head.

In the painting we are examining at the moment, although the nude is in the centre of the picture, the fixed point is the chair. The green of the chair plus the yellow lines give us the colour of the walls. The floor is red, which complements the green.

If we mix red with green we get the colour of the decorations, the window frame, the dark vertical patch on the left and the shadow of the figure on the chair. Through the window we can see the bright blue of the sky. If we mix this blue with some green and some red, we get the colour used for the bluish line between the floor and the wall on the right-hand side.

If we now look at the figure, we find that what seems a natural pose is in fact the result of careful study. The colours and rhythm of the whole composition are deliberate. Try finding the different construction lines by putting a piece of tracing paper over the top and repeating the exercise we did for Ingres.

The Nude and Nature by František Kupka

In a study of the artistic behaviour of apes and its relationship with human art, Desmond Morris wrote:

"The art world has seen a whole series of reactions against the traditional communicative functions of art. As a result, painting has been

ome more and more abstract and has intention-
lly returned to a stage similar to that of the
rimates or, in other words, pure aesthetic experi-
nentation."

he first painters to move towards abstraction
ere originally strictly figurative artists. Fran-
šek Kupka was one example. He was born in
zechoslovakia in 1871 and studied at the School
f Fine Arts in Prague and later in Vienna. After
avelling widely in Europe he settled in Paris
here he earned a living by illustrating books and
naking satirical drawings for newspapers. In
906 he withdrew to Puteaux on the outskirts of
aris to live a life of solitude. At the outset he was
afluenced by symbolism, Fauvism and Cubism
he Section d'Or, one of the driving forces behind
ubism, was based in Puteaux), but then began to
evote himself to abstract art.

ifficult years followed, since František Kupka
ad chosen a lonely, unpopular road, but he fi-
ally emerged as one of the great pioneers of
bstract art.

ollowing a procedure similar to that used by
elaunay, Kupka broke down figurative elements
nto planes of colour, which he then steadily elim-
nated to give rise to pure orchestration of colour.
he figurative element was replaced by autono-
ous ellipses of pure colour. Apollinaire was
later to coin the term "Orphism" for this style of
painting, an allusion to its rhythmical, musical
qualities.

Kupka's art moved in two different directions:
towards constructivism on the one hand and
towards chromatic expressionism on the other.
Very few exhibitions of his work were held during
his lifetime, but after his death a large retrospec-
tive exhibition was organized in the Museum of
Modern Art in Paris (1958).

Let us take a look at one of Kupka's figurative
paintings, dated 1903, on page 68. Before our
attention is attracted by the figure, we are struck
by the movement of the waves. The composition
of the painting appears to follow a highly original
pattern of movement. The painting is developed
spirally, in a kind of ellipsis, something we find
later in Kupka's abstract works. The emotions
aroused by the painting are the result not of the
figure in the centre but of the universe revolving
around the figure. The woman is a spectator of the
powerful forces which could carry her away at any
moment. Her pose further enhances the idea of her
fragility.

Twenty years later Kupka painted *Blue in Movement* (on page 69). The figure is replaced by
vortices of colour which, like the waves, appear
to be about to swallow us up.

*ft: František Kupka
871-1957): Vlna, 1903 –
l on canvas, 100 × 145
a – Museum of
ne Arts, Ostrava*

*antišek Kupka:
ue in Movement, 1923 –
rodni Gallery, Prague*

69

Piet Mondrian's Nudes

When the futurists declared that art was dead they forgot to point out that the art critics had died the day before to help it on its way. Though the role of the art critic has changed radically since then, it is still the critic's prerogative to heap praise or blame upon a certain painting or painter. Listen to what Michel Senphor wrote about the critics in his biography of Piet Mondrian:

"In January 1909 the exhibition held by the trio Spoor-Sluyters-Mondrian at the Municipal Gallery in Amsterdam led to an outcry in the Dutch press. Most of the criticism was directed against Mondrian. He had exhibited a series of new canvases depicting Zeeland and some other earlier paintings of Brabant. Most of them were large sketches made on unprepared board, with large areas completely bare. All the 'great names' came out in force to attack Mondrian: famous writers, writers trying to become famous, well-known journalists and art critics, experts on what was considered good taste. Lesser-known critics were generally more prudent, saying that maybe they had not understood properly. On the whole, they served the history of art better than their more illustrious colleagues. The great writer Frederik van Eeden, for example, in an article for a ma-gazine (*Health and Decay in Art*), said that 'i Mondrian the decline is tragic and terrible; h original talents were so great that he had farthe to fall. Some of his early paintings are truly ma nificent and his vision of nature is grandiose an noble. At times his use of colour is marvellou But there is no trace of all this in his latest work Who or what has made him lose his head? Prol ably Van Gogh. It is in any case clear tha whatever the reason may be, he has totally lost h balance and has begun scribbling in an abom nable way'. Later, still referring to Mondrian, h speaks of stupidity and lack of sensibility.

Israel Quiérido, another great Dutch novelis agrees with Van Eeden: Mondrian, according t Quiérido, is sick, even degenerate. A few yea later Erich Wichmann wrote: 'Mondrian? just beautiful corpse'. Just Havelaar, a famous essa ist and intellectual, said that 'Mondrian has nev been a very good painter' (*Het Vaderland*, Marc 8, 1922).

In 1910, a year after the Exhibition, Mondria made an important contribution to the Lumini exhibition, again in the Municipal Gallery Amsterdam. Once more, he became the object the critics' wrath. N.H. Wolf, a very well-know critic who also claimed to be a friend Mondrian, wrote that 'his work is that of a sic

erson, someone who is not normal', adding that
t is not even art any more'."

nyone who loves art also loves nature. We get
e same thrill from gazing at a landscape bathed
 full sunshine or in a certain light as we get from
oking at a picture painted, say, by one of the
npressionists. One day, a few years ago, as I
andered around the countryside looking for in-
piration for a painting, totally inundated by the
ensations that only nature can give, I bent down
 pick up a small leaf of a pear tree. The leaf was
val and curved slightly inward and its colours
anged from green to red with small brown
atches. That tiny leaf contained all the shades of
utumn. That well-known shape and those hues
eemed to me to represent an entire landscape.
hat day I gathered stones, leaves and roots. I felt
e same sensation later on looking at paintings
y Kandisky, Klee and Mondrian; I began to
nderstand what abstract art was all about.

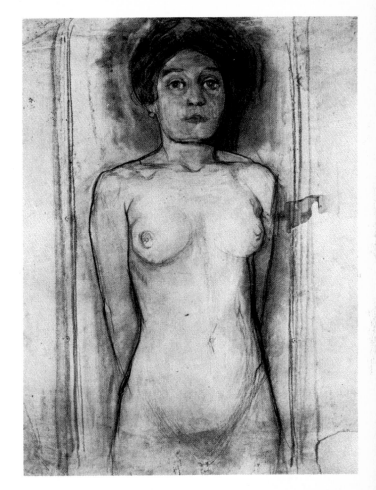

et Mondrian (1872-1944): Nude, *1908-1911 – black chalk,*
× 42 cm – Gemeentemuseum, The Hague

Now let us take a look at the first nude painting by Mondrian.

It is a black chalk drawing on straw-paper carried out with great skill and portrays a female figure leaning against a narrow door, perhaps the door of a cupboard. The anatomical construction is very clear and the lines in the shaded areas outline the muscles.

Mondrian's second nude is entitled *Spring* and manages to express more sensations than the first. The figure is drawn by means of a sequence of wavy lines which are then repeated in the space external to the figure itself, thus creating the sensation of something growing vertically upward while being blown horizontally by a light breeze exactly like a spring flower in a field.

A third study by Mondrian concludes this journey towards abstraction (on page 73).

In this painting we can still recognize the general image of the first. The one eye is balanced by the sensation of the other looking out into the un-

Piet Mondrian: Spring, *ca. 1905 – charcoal on cardboard, 69.5 × 46 cm – Slijper Collection, Blaricum*

72

shaded area. It feels as if the inner soul of the figure is looking out to discover what lies beyond her body. The body itself is made up of coloured blocks which become rhythmical squares. The construction lines lead through various shades of grey to the bottom of the picture which thus dominates. The figure emerges from the semi-darkness and her soul appears to be deciding whether to come out into the light or go back into the dark.

Van Gogh's Nudes

When I look at Van Gogh's paintings I can't help feeling strange sensations, such as for example feeling a sense of shame for his contemporaries who didn't understand him and didn't realize what a great painter he was. Is this the reason, I very often ask myself, why nowadays his paintings are sold for such enormous sums of money? Another sensation is the one I feel when I read the numerous letters that Van Gogh wrote to his

Piet Mondrian: Nude, *1912 – oil on canvas, 140 × 98 cm – Gemeentemuseum – Blaricum, Slijper Loan, The Hague*

brother Théo: it is the exhaustation due to the continuous efforts to be accepted and loved first as human being, preacher and painter. If we read the letter found in his pocket on July 29, 1890 (when he committed suicide), we are aware of the way such an exhaustation had already killed him, even before he shot himself.

"Dearest brother,

Thank you for your most welcome letter and for the 50 Fr. note inside it. I should like to write and tell you about lots of things, but I realize it would be useless. I hope you found those people favourably disposed towards you.

It wasn't necessary for you to reassure me as to the tranquillity of your family life. I think I have seen the good and the bad side of it – on the other hand, I agree that bringing up a kid in a fourth-floor apartment is absolute slavery, both for you and for Jo. As long as everything is going well, which is what matters, because I should insist on things of minor importance, upon my word, it will be a long time before there is any possibility of discussing business with a more serene mind. That's the only thing I can say for the moment. For my part, I have noted this with a certain amount of alarm and I am still not over it. But for the moment that is all. The other painters, whatever they may think, instinctively keep their

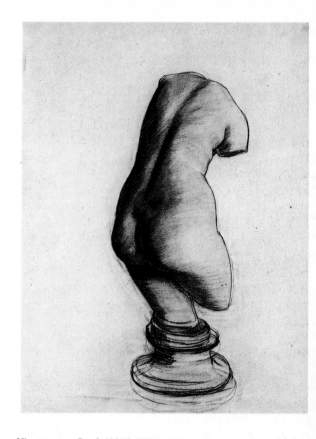

Vincent van Gogh (1853-1890): Plaster Statuette, Seen from behind – *Paris, April-June 1886 – charcoal, 61 × 45 cm – Rjiksmuseum Vincent van Gogh, Amsterdam*

distance from any discussions about business nowadays.

Besides, it's true, all we can do is let our paintings speak for us.

And yet, my dear brother, as I have told you time and time again and will repeat once more with all the good intentions that can come from a mind aimed constantly at doing as much good as possible – I want to say once again that I have always thought of you as something more than a mere dealer of Corot's paintings and that, through me, you have taken part in actually producing a number of paintings, which, although a total failure, still retain their serenity. Because that's how things stand and that is all, or at least the main thing that I can say at this moment of relative crisis. At a moment in which things between dealers in dead artists' paintings and live artists' paintings are very tense.

Well, I risk my life in my work and I'm already half out of my mind, – all right – but you're not a dealer in human beings, as far as I know, and it seems to me that you are free to make your decision, really behaving with humanity, but what in Heaven's name do you want?"

Another sensation is that of frenzy. When Vincent decided to become a painter he threw himself into his work so assiduously and with such a frenzy as

Vincent van Gogh: Plaster Statuette, *April- June 1886 – oil on canvas, 41 × 32.5 cm – Rijksmuseum Vincent van Gogh, Amsterdam*

to frighten anyone who came near him. At the beginning, Van Gogh did not like the Impressionists and wrote in a letter to his sister:

"Everything you hope for – to attain independence in your work, to influence others – vanishes into nothing, absolutely nothing.

And yet painting a picture gives a certain amount of joy, though at this moment there are about twenty painters here – all of whom have more debts than money and lead a life comparable to that of a stray dog – who are, however, probably more important than the whole official exhibition as far as future pictorial style is concerned. I think that the essential feature of a painter is knowing how to paint. Knowing how to paint, knowing how to paint better, is the beginning of something that will go on for many years; it will continue to last as long as there are eyes capable of enjoying something which is particularly beautiful. Although I regret that by working harder you don't get any richer – on the contrary....

If only you could, you could get a lot more done, join up with the others, or something. Because nowadays everybody is tied up to the chances of earning their daily bread, which means that in fact they are anything but free.

You ask me if I have sent anything to the 'Arts' exhibition – certainly not! The only trouble is that

Théo sent Mr. Tersteeg a group of paintings by impressionist artists and some of mine happened to be among them. The only result was, according to what Théo told me, that neither Tersteeg nor the artists saw anything in them.

Well, that is quite understandable, because it is always the same thing. You hear a lot of talk about impressionist paintings, you expect them to be something fantastic, and... then when you see them for the first time they are bitterly disappointing. They look dull, decidedly unattractive, badly painted, badly drawn, with awful colours, in short, they couldn't be worse.

That was my first impression when I came to Paris, imbued as I was with the ideas of Mauve, Israels and other skilled painters. When they hold exhibitions of only impressionists in Paris, I think many visitors go away bitterly disappointed and even indignant."

He tried to improve his drawing academically by attending various schools, but his impetuosity and desire to cut corners turned what should have been a gradual pictorial maturity into a sort of all-in wrestling match.

Vincent worked for a short while in Cormon's "atelier," but, as he himself said in a letter to his English friend and fellow painter Levens, he resisted only three or four months:

"I was in Cormon's studio for three or four months but I didn't find it as useful as I had thought it might be. Perhaps it was my fault. Anyway, I left, as I did in Antwerp, and since then I have been working on my own and feeling myself again ...."

In Cormon's studio Vincent had to copy classical plaster statues. The method was the usual one described earlier in this book: to make various pencil, charcoal, oil or watercolour sketches of the statue from different points of view in an attempt to make a complete study of the statue from all possible angles.

The first study we see on page 74 has been drawn in charcoal with lighting coming from the side to highlight the muscles on the left-hand side of the back. The shading has been done hurriedly without taking the trouble to make corrections. Generally speaking, painters' studies and sketches are much more spontaneous than oil paintings.

This, however, was not the case with the Impressionists since they thought of their studies as having the same value as paintings. This can be seen in the oil study on page 75: it has been done in the same "spirit" as the sketch, working with quick strokes of the brush. The result is that both works have an inner tension so that an academic plaster statue becomes the sensuous body of a peasant woman, ready to face grief and happiness with equal courage.

The popular image of artists is very much based on impressionist painters. Many of them led difficult, unhappy lives and very few of them were able to live off the rewards of their work in their old age.

Through the letters they wrote to friends and fellow artists, we often discover that they were weak characters, unable to cope with the prejudiced attitudes of their day.

We think, for example, of Toulouse-Lautrec, whose portraits are now bought for hundreds of thousands of dollars by the descendants of the "respectable" bourgeoisie the artist shocked in his day. Toulouse-Lautrec, an alcoholic, died young. He was a weak man and this is the case with many innovative artists.

Their weakness is directly proportional to their artistic sensibility. I have never seen a strong man crying with joy at the sight of a cornfield with poppies at twilight.

Nearly all the world's great paintings are the work of men with fragile, generous hearts, like Leonardo da Vinci, Michelangelo, Caravaggio, Corot, Cézanne, Van Gogh and Gauguin.

Paul Gauguin

Paul Gauguin (1848-1903) started to paint relatively late in life, after giving up a promising career as a banker. Van Gogh persuaded him to live with him for some time, in the belief that this would lead to a kind of artistic brotherhood similar to the Pre-Raphaelite Brotherhood in England.

Unfortunately their relationship turned out to be a tragic one. Gauguin returned to Paris and shortly afterwards decided to go to live on an island in the South Pacific. He believed that art was in serious danger of losing its inner emotional intensity and capacity for immediate expression.

Early in his artistic life Gauguin had spent a period in Brittany studying rural art and it was here that he began to take an interest in primitive art and religious primitivism. He was convinced that he could turn colour into a universal, artistic language.

To save his artistic soul, he felt he had to leave Europe and live among the natives of the South Seas. The works he brought back from the South Pacific puzzled almost everyone. They were considered wild and primitive, hardly surprising if one remembers that in his attempt to understand the natives he often copied their works of art. To simplify the outlines of his figures he used patches of violent colour. Feeling that his work would never be understood in Europe he returned to his beloved South Sea islands where he died of hardship and loneliness.

Gauguin systematically tried to hide his own weakness by creating his own genre of painting to love and to defend at all costs. This did not turn him into a "strong" man but it made him sure of what he was doing and gave him the strength to go on doing it until the end.

The Spirits of the Dead, by Paul Gauguin

In 1863 Manet painted Olympia, whose white skin contrasted with the dark skin of her maidservant. In 1893 Gauguin "replaced" Olympia with a wonderful young Tahitian girl whose skin is the colour of newly ploughed earth. Like Olympia, the girl is inviting us to make love. But the girl's brown body lying on a white sheet against a blue and violet background, with a figure representing death on the left-hand side, is also a kind of warning, reminding man of the inevitability of the sequence love/life/death. The natural order of things cannot be changed.

The composition of the painting is very simple: a figure lying diagonally across a white bed against

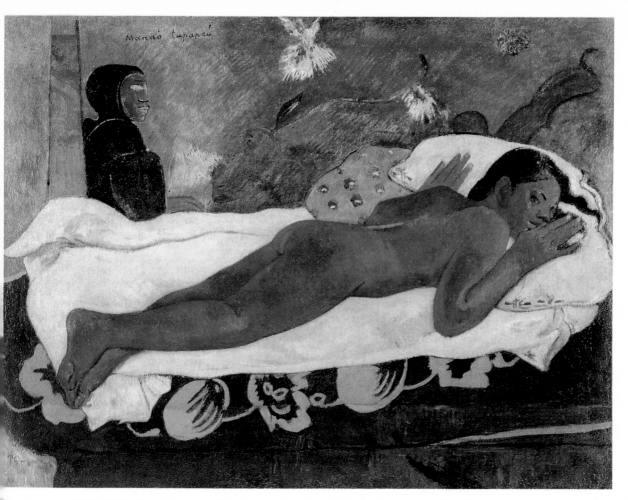

Paul Gauguin (1848-1903): Manaò Tupapaù: The Spirits of the Dead, *1892 – oil on canvas, 73 × 92 cm –*
Albright Knox Art Gallery – A. Conger Goodyear Collection, Buffalo

Luisella Lissoni:
Rotation of a Plaster
Statue of a Bust –
chalk on pouncing
paper

dark background on which a beam and the idol re positioned vertically.

auguin paints in great masses of colour, a combination of Pissarro and the study of Japanese rints. The result is an essentiality that was to ave an enormous influence on future painting, specially that of Munch who saw in Gauguin's ainting the starting point for his own desperately xpressionistic art.

rawing Studies of the Rotation of a Plaster tatue of a Bust, following Luisella Lissoni

Before copying her model from real life, Luisella nade a few sketches of the rotation of plaster tatues. The first is the one on the right, seen from ne front; the second is the one on the left, showng the back of the bust, and the third is the profile n the middle.

'he drawings are done on pouncing paper, which recommend for pastel and charcoal drawings. f you look carefully at a plaster cast you will see hat the white of the statue absorbs the colours of urrounding objects; if, for example, there is a vooden cupboard near the statue, it will tend to e slightly brown in colour. For her drawings uisella used a soft, 6B pencil. Then she shaded n the darker areas with grey chalk, smudging it

slightly with her fingers or with a stump. She used white chalk to create the areas of light. Remember that the white must be blended with the grey of the shaded parts; for perfect results rub the tip of the thumb lightly over the chalk. After outlining all the shapes with a sharp pastel, make a wide cross-hatching. When drawing plaster statues, always colour the background to create extra volume and give added vitality to the composition. In my opinion the best kind of statue to use is a bust of a female nude. This particular one was done in the 1930-40s by a highly skilled minor sculptor. It was first modelled from life in clay and was used by artists who could not afford to pay a real model. Casts of classical statues are the safest from the anatomical point of view; if these are impossible to find, check the anatomical structure very carefully before purchasing the statue.

Vallotton and Japanese Art

Félix Vallotton was born in Lausanne in 1865. At the age of seventeen he went to Paris and was to live and work there all his life. He attended the Académie Julian and explored his artistic talent by copying works by Dürer, Holbein and Rembrandt in the Louvre. Up to 1890 his work, though original and formally correct, had little in common with that of the post-impressionist avant-garde. Then he joined the Nabis group and learned the basic rules of two-dimensional composition and arabesque. He rejected symbolism in favour of the representation of everyday life and objects. His wood-engravings, most of which can be dated to the period 1892-1897, when he gave up painting, are based on scenes of everyday life. When he returned to painting, his favourite subjects were interiors, nudes and landscapes, painted using bright, pure colours like those used in later years by the surrealists. Vallotton died in Paris in 1925.

Vallotton's relationship with Japanese art, and with wood engravings in particular, is worthy of special mention. Vallotton, like Gauguin, Van Gogh and the other artists in the Nabis group, possessed a small collection of Oriental art. It is difficult to fully understand some of his engravings without taking account of the influence of certain Japanese prints, especially those of Hokusai.

It should be remembered that Vallotton worked only in black and white, which makes the contents and form of the works more intense. One of the most striking aspects of the engravings is the way in which the two colours are clearly separated, so that there is a high concentration of contrast in each of the small works. The decorative element (see *La Paresse*, for example) is composed of system of dots, rose cuts, squares and lines which respect the volume of the subject-matter and create the illusion of space without representing real third dimension. The effect is a kind of austere, archaic elegance which becomes the hallmark of Vallotton's engravings. The negative background produces positive effects. The horizontal and vertical structure of the woodcuts, with the help of objects and figures cut from the frame enables Vallotton to heighten the emotional intensity of the scene.

Vallotton often uses barriers, lattices or vertical lines where black and white alternate, thus relegating the figure to second place and giving prominence to the purely decorative elements.

But it is logical now to take into consideration wood engraving and give examples of the most important stages of such a technique.

Félix Vallotton (1865-1925): La Paresse, *1896 – wood engraving, 17.7 × 12.2 cm – Museum of Fine Arts, Lausanne*

How to Cut Wood for Wood Engravings

The tools used to make wood engravings are miniature gouges. Their points have different shapes

in order to make differently- shaped cuts. The gouges are fitted onto a round handle, one side of which is flat. This makes it easier to grip in the correct working position.

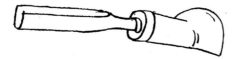

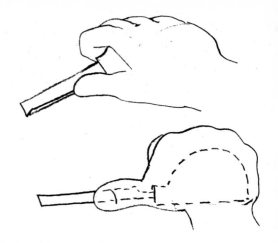

The gouge is gripped like a potato peeler, with the thumb resting firmly on the blade. The angle formed by the blade and the wood is generally very small (maximum 10-20 degrees). If you hold it at this angle, the gouge will just chip the wood lightly, leaving a delicate impression like a brush stroke. If the working angle is too high, the gouge will make a deep cut and will be difficult to control. If the angle is too low, the blade will slip on the wood. To prevent slipping, press lightly on the blade with the index and middle fingers of the left hand.

The type of wood used for wood-engravings is the end grain of pear or cherry wood. If we take a piece of wood we can see that there is a wider part on which we can see the patterns of the grain.

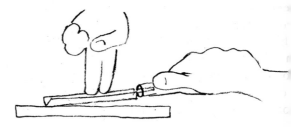

84

we cut lengthwise along the grain the gouge will make a normal impression, whereas, if we cut against the grain the gouge will split the wood. This method is used by Expressionist painters to give their woodcuts a more dramatic effect.) Let us now take a look at the smaller end – the part where it was sawn off and where we can see the

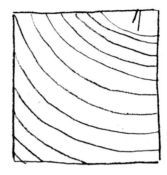

concentric annual growth rings. This is end grain wood. The structure of the fibres of wood taken from this part enables us to cut it easily in all directions.

The wood must be perfectly smooth and gripped gently in a special vice specifically designed for wood engravers.

This consists of a board or plank secured to a table in which threaded holes have been made in a horizontal and vertical direction. There are also wooden brackets which can be screwed into the holes in any desired position.

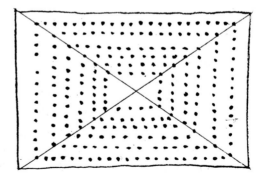

After having completed your drawing, transfer it onto tracing paper and then prick all the outlines with a pin. Using a paint brush, cover the surface of the wood with a uniform coat of black chin ink. Place the tracing paper on the wood with th drawing face down so that the pencil marks are i

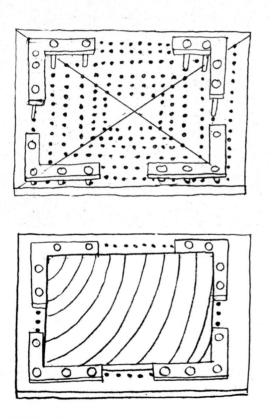

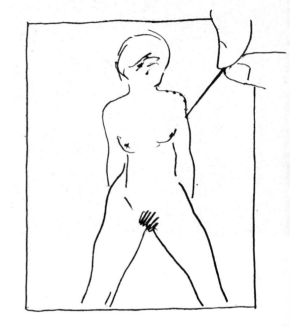

direct contact with the wood. Secure it in plac with adhesive tape. Go over the holes with ord nary white chalk. When you lift the paper, yo will see a series of small white dots on the woo

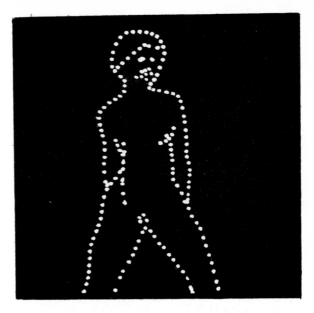

which will give you the outline of the drawing. The chalk outline must be fixed with a fixative otherwise it will disappear. Follow the dots with a white pencil to reconstruct the whole drawing. Fix again and then proceed with the engraving. Remember that everything you want to appear white when printed must be gouged out and the black must be left in relief. The china ink background will help you to see the drawing more clearly. If you have to cut a line or a circle you will instinctively want to start from the point nearest you and work outwards. This is wrong. The ideal is to work backwards a little bit at a time (see the example on page 88) both for circles and for curves.

Making such a long cut in one go is risky, especially for the novice. You could very easily ruin the drawing or obtain uneven lines.

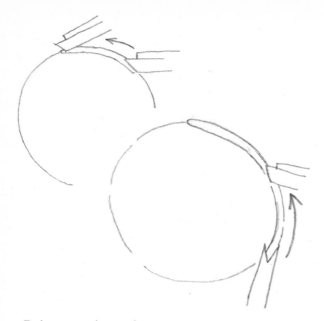

Remember that the engraving will be the revers
of the drawing but will come out the right wa
when printed.

You really need a press to print properly, but wit
a little patience it is also possible to print by han
using a spoon- shaped modelling spatula.

Use Japanese rice paper, ink with an ink roller an
spread the ink (which is sold in tubes) over a ver

Below are the various types of cuts that can be
achieved with a gouge.

Nowadays, this technique is also used for engrav-

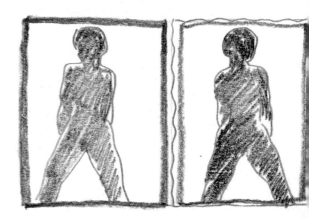

ings on linoleum, known as linocuts. After having
completed the engraving it can be printed.

thick plate of glass or marble, using first a hori
zontal movement and then a vertical one.

When the ink has formed a thin layer over th
entire surface, you can begin to ink your cliché by

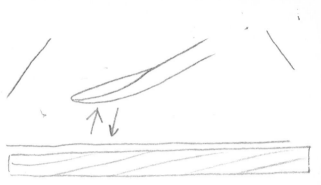

running the roller very gently over the raised part of the engraving.

When it is evenly inked all over, place the paper carefully over the cliché and then, using the tip of the modelling spatula, rub gently over the entire raised surface without pressing too hard.

If the spatula should 'stick' while you are working, dip it in talcum powder before rubbing.

Lift off the sheet of paper and hang it on a line with two clips for 24 hours to allow the ink to dry.

Ineluctably Bound, by Franco Tripodi

Some time ago I asked my friend and fellow painter Franco Tripodi if he could give me some material for publication in this book. I also asked him if I could watch him at work on one of his paintings.

Tripodi is a young artist who works with the humility of a Renaissance painter. Every one of his paintings is the result of slow, painstaking work as every good painting should be.

The work starts with a preliminary drawing, comparable to one of the cartoons of old. Then, on a large board, Tripodi prepares a "bed" of clay, on which he creates feverishly calculated "shapes" in bas-relief. Then something happens to the basrelief. Something comparable to its fate with the passing of time: as the clay dries it forms fractures and cracks, rather like the arid, sun-baked shores of an African river. Now this matrix-mother is ready to generate beyond herself. Tripodi continues working, like a mosaicist, with the confident and accurate movements of someone who has tried out and improved those movements thousands of times before until he has succeeded in reaching perfection.

He cuts and rips up some small squares of canvas or gauze. He prepares a binder using rabbit or fish glue (available in shops in the form of granules or flakes). Rabbit glue is a strong glue and fish glue is more delicate. He mixes them together using two-thirds rabbit glue and one-third fish glue. He lets the glue soak for a few hours, leaves it to boil in a double boiler until it has completely dissolved and then uses it still hot in proportions of about 20 grams per litre of water. To obtain a stronger glue he simply uses less water.

He dips the squares into the glue, one at a time, and presses them onto the matrix and then dabs the still sticky canvas with a stiff brush impregnated with completely dry powdered paint. This pigment is absorbed and in the areas where there are cracks the colour deposits in greater quantities, giving that stupendous effect typical of this kind of painting. Once the canvas has dried completely it can be removed and will maintain the shape of a basrelief. These paintings, and especially *Ineluctably Bound*, are achieved by means of stages and operations which create a sort of stratification of

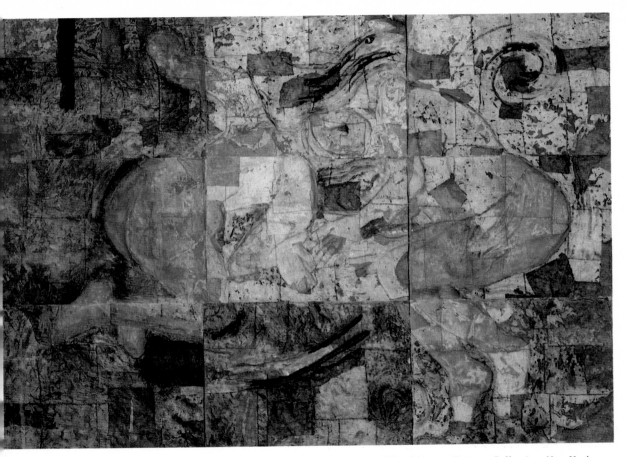

Franco Tripodi: Ineluctably Bound, *1985 – relief, pigments and oil on canvas, 150 × 210 cm – Private Collection, New York*

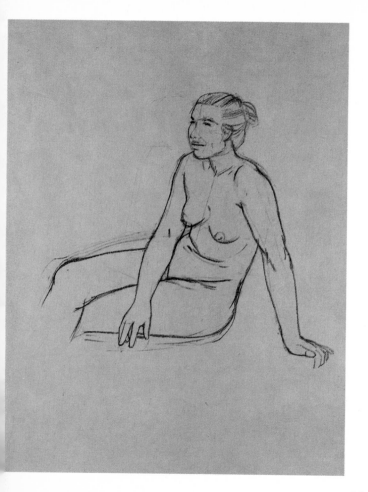

materials and techniques, which range from sculpture to painting. The idea, which is defined in the drawing, follows an almost obligatory path; the stratifications of the materials are also in the mind. The clay – says Tripodi – is alive during the transition phase leading up to the painting: it contracts, it shatters. These movements are highlighted by the "seams" of the squares of canvas and gauze which mingle to create transparencies with the all-important contribution of the natural pigments. Consequently – Tripodi concludes – it is always the earth that reappears on the surface. The final effect is that of a painted bas-relief: it is as though the figures are frozen and intentionally suspended in abstract space.

Line Drawings of Nudes

It is not easy to make line drawings of nudes. Even great artists rarely use this technique to any great extent until relatively late in their careers. The impression of volume has to be rendered by lines alone without using chiaroscuro effects. The drawing shown here is a charcoal drawing on the rough side of a piece of ordinary wrapping paper. After making a rough sketch of the figure pressing very lightly with the charcoal, I tried to draw the outline of the body by tracing the lines joining the points where muscles cross (or, in other words, the points where shadows are formed). When making a line drawing you have always to try to be as synthetic as possible, eliminating any details that are superfluous. If, for example, there are several folds on the belly, only the most obvious ones are drawn. Chiaroscuro drawings, on the other hand, are necessarily detailed.

Line drawing takes us into a completely different world, the world of expressive lines. Painters use line drawings as a way of discovering what is absolutely essential and what can be left out without ruining the sense of volume.

The Meaning of a Figure

If you read Freud you will find that he often uses painting to back up his theories. He discovered, for example, that artists, and painters in particular, were able to understand the human soul. In order to give expression to the feelings of the person being painted, a painter must know the meaning of certain gestures, facial expressions or movements of the hands and body. A portrait painter must be able to understand a person's inner feelings by looking at his face. Often when people have a smile on their faces, their eyes can

still betray deep sadness; even when we see moving figures, it is sometimes possible to detect worry or loneliness from the position of the head or the movement of the arms.

We have to learn to observe people as the great Leonardo da Vinci used to do. He often followed his models around for days in order to gain greater insight into their inner feelings.

In a way, Freud merely gave scientific confirmation to something that all good painters already knew.

People often adopt certain attitudes in an attempt to hide others. With careful observation, however, it is always possible to see through them.

Painters may thus paint one thing while really expressing another.

This is true of almost all the figurative art of the past, where the source of inspiration was generally a sacred symbol. Towards the end of the 19th century and at the beginning of the 20th, the symbol became something from real life. In abstract painting, on the other hand, the symbol is no longer the 'significatum', or meaning, of the painting at all and the artist is completely free to express only the 'signifier.'

When an impressionist painter gave his work a title such as *Still Life with Clock*, we could feel sure that in the painting we would find all the elements that gave the painting its title.

If Kandinsky called a painting *Blue Sky*, we were sure at least of finding organic elements giving us the sensation of flying in the sky like balloons.

Over the last thirty years or so things have changed. The titles given to pictures are merely sounds with no real reference to what we actually see. This is clearly not right and something must be done to redress the balance in future.

We must not forget that in addition to being wonderful craftsmen the artists of the past were also learned men. Their learning was the result of their inborn curiosity.

Rodin realized that artistic vibration could be achieved through pencil drawings and in fact his drawings, done with the impetuous strokes of an artist accustomed to working with stone, anticipate certain techniques we later find in the works of Klimt and Schiele.

To achieve this kind of fluidity, Rodin made enormous sacrifices.

The writer Rainer Maria Rilke, who became Rodin's secretary, had this to say in the book he wrote about the great sculptor:

"Then the war came and Rodin went to Brussels, working whenever he could. He did some sculptures for private houses, others for the Stock Exchange building and he also created the four large statues that stand at the corners of the monument to the burgomaster Loos in Antwerp Park. He worked conscientiously on all these jobs, without ever letting his real personality show through.

At the same time, however, he developed his real artistic personality during leisure hours, during the evenings or in the calm of the night and thus, for years, his energy was being consumed on two fronts. He had the strength of someone waiting to create a masterpiece, the silent resistance of great men.

He looked for truth wherever he was and found it at the most unlikely moments and in the most unlikely places. For years he went on searching humbly, like a beginner.

Nobody understood what he was doing or what he was going through; he confided in nobody and had hardly any friends. He hid behind the work he had to perform to earn a living and waited for the time when he could create his masterpieces. He read a lot. It was normal to see him walking through the streets of Brussels with a book in his hand ...".

The drawing we are going to look at now is by Rodin. In my opinion it was drawn from memory, something which is quite easy for a painter or sculptor who is familiar with the human figure, especially if the figure in question is a loved one. Rodin's drawing is of a female figure, perhaps a woman he

Auguste Rodin (1840-1917): Lying Nude –
graphite and watercolour on paper, 21.5 × 26 cm –
Rodin Museum, Paris

loved or a woman he wished to make immortal through his art.

The outline is drawn firmly and confidently, with a soft, vibrant touch. The muscles are seen as generating movement rather than being drawn in anatomically perfect fashion.

Rodin, the perfect innovator, manages to draw with no frills or affectation, creating a spontaneity that will often be imitated but never equalled.

Now let's try to see what practical lessons we can learn from this. It is important to have a good visual memory and the only way to acquire one is by drawing a lot. You therefore have to love drawing and practise whenever you can by copying what you see. Among my old notes and sketches I have found two drawings which may illustrate a few useful points. The first is a sketch I drew to show my model the pose I wanted her to take up. It was done in a hurry and is extremely basic. Note how the drawing has the air of a finished work, despite the fact that it was done at great speed.

Taken by themselves, the head and the hands would have no anatomical significance whatsoever and yet in the context of the drawing they convey the idea of the volume of the hair and the hand seen in perspective.

You should try to make as many sketches of this sort as possible, perhaps by drawing people lying on the beach. This is the only way to learn how to make quick sketches by drawing only what is strictly necessary.

The second drawing we are going to look at is one I did in the 1970s as an attack on hyper-realism, which I consider to be a commercial fad having more in common with illustration than with art.

The figure was drawn in pencil like the previous one but then I added some watercolour to give colour to the skin. The colour was obtained by mixing yellow ochre with vermilion, using a lot of water. Diluted bistre was then used for the hair.

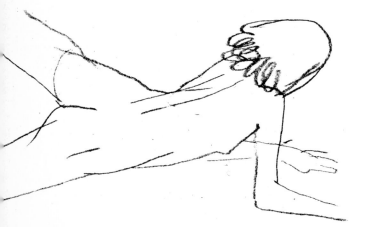

Remember that bistre is the result of mixing equal
quantities of carmine, ultramarine blue and cadmium yellow.
Obviously this kind of work can only be done by
experienced painters.
So try not to get depressed if your first attempts
are not a success. Keep trying. You will never
learn unless you persist.

La Toilette, by Camille Corot

Camille Corot was born in Paris in 1796. His father worked in the textile trade and his mother was a dressmaker. Before his dream of becoming a painter came true, Corot was apprenticed to two textile merchants. In 1822 his father finally gave him permission to follow his artistic vocation and also agreed to send his son a monthly sum to enable him to work without too many financial worries. Corot's training was neo-classical: he listened to the advice given to him by Michallon and at the same time dreamed of travelling to Italy. After a long journey through Switzerland and Italy Corot finally arrived in Rome in 1825. When he returned to Paris in 1828, he took with him a series of landscapes rightly considered to be among the very best paintings of the whole of the 19th century. Volterra, Venice, the Roman castles, the Sabine hills – Corot managed to make even the most difficult landscapes look beautifully familiar. Although his basic vision belonged to the 18th century, there was something completely new in the young artist's large compositions: the combination of landscapes and realism. When his works were exhibited at the Salon in 1827, the critics were divided: many failed to see anything new in the pictures at all. Corot was not disheartened. He continued travelling and painting, learning an improving all the time. From 1829 onwards h divided his time between Fontainebleau and No mandy, painting in Paris and in Rouen. He mad a second trip to Italy in 1834, visiting Genoa, Pis and Florence. His father died in 1847 and in th following year his *Corner of Italy* was bought b the State and exhibited in the Museum of Doua In 1851 he made the first of many visits to Arra where his friend Dutilleux lived. In 1855 his pain ings were exhibited at the Universal Exhibitio and were greatly admired. In 1861 Berthe Moriso became a pupil of his. The Emperor Napoleo bought several of his paintings for his private co lection and a few years later Corot was electe member of the jury for the Salon. He continued travel a lot, though his favourite place was sti Fontainebleau. He died in the Ville d'Avray a Isle-Adam on February 22, 1875.

When Camille Corot was already an establishe painter, he learned that the well-known litho grapher and caricaturist Honoré Daumier ha become blind and was living in poverty. Wit great generosity, Corot gave Daumier his house i the country, so that he could end his days in dignified manner. Why do I bother to mention thi episode which in a way is quite marginal to th life of Corot? Probably because it shows a sens

of solidarity, unselfishness and idealism that appear somewhat anachronistic in our modern world. Corot was always surrounded by his pupils and other young artists who nicknamed him "père Corot." Real art means solidarity, communion and love for others, though today this seems to have been completely forgotten. But let's not digress too much; let's try to get to know Corot through his works and, in particular, his landscapes.

Corot's predilection for landscapes was a conscious artistic decision. The light he was always looking for and which he managed to put into his pictures acted as a "beacon" for the Impressionists who followed him. Even when painting figures, however, he managed to create a wonderful sense of atmosphere, as in the example shown here which he called *Landscape with Figures* though it later became known as *La Toilette*. It should be remembered that the critics were not always on Corot's side and at times attacked him quite vehemently. This was in fact one of the reasons why he finally decided to retire to the forest of Fontainebleau, where he was able to paint in peace. He was soon joined there by many other great artists of the day.

Taking a closer look at the painting I have just

Camille Corot (1796-1875): La Toilette, 1859 – oil on canvas, 179 × 92 cm – Private Collection, Paris

mentioned, we notice the marvellous logic which lies behind the composition. The rhythm depends not on the figure but on the movement of the tree trunks which form a sequence of triangles. The sensations conveyed by the painting are the result of the precision of its composition. We shall see something similar to this later on when we look at the work of Giacomo Balla. Always try to analyze paintings from the point of view of the logic of their structural composition.

Maurice de Vlaminck

I have always been particularly fond of Maurice de Vlaminck and his anarchic tendencies. Here we are going to examine one of his engravings, comparing it to those of Vallotton. The first thing we notice is that the outline of the figures is not drawn in tidy, clear-cut lines as in Vallotton's work. The outline is vibrant and uneven, performed with one cut of the gouge, taking full advantage of the way the knife tears the fibres of the wood.

Vlaminck's writings are full of irony and so are his pictures. In this woodcut the central figure is taking off his mask with his left hand (on the right as you look at the picture), covering up a part of his face. The face and the mask are the same person. But this is not all: the figure on the left also appears to have the same face as the mask. I am not sure whethe this is done on purpose or accidentally; knowin Vlaminck either could be possible.

In art there is no such thing as a completely ration or a completely irrational painter: both these ten dencies must coexist side by side. The importar thing is knowing how to blend the two. Artists lik Paul Klee or Kandinsky who wrote about art (Th Theory of Form and Representation by Klee an Dots, Lines and Surfaces and Spirituality in Art b Kandinsky) were no more rational when paintin than Van Gogh or Delacroix. Artists often put thei thoughts into words. It is only the greed of other that turns these thoughts into theories.

Maurice de Vlaminck was born in Paris on Apri 4, 1876. His father was a Catholic of Flemis origin (though he did not practise his religion) while his mother, who looked after her son's re ligious education, was a Protestant from Lorraine Vlaminck was not a good student and once wrot of himself: "I was not one of those studious pupil who do well in examinations." In 1893 he too drawing lessons with a certain Robichon, a mem ber of the Société des Artistes Français. Vlaminc wrote: "I drew for myself and for no one else.... was 17 and like many other boys of my age I wrot poems about life, sometimes dedicated to th woman I was never to meet." In 1894, at the ag

f eighteen, he married Susanne Berly. He earned
poor living by giving violin lessons, sometimes
aking part in cycling or rowing races hoping to
vin enough money to make ends meet. In 1896 he
eft to do military service. He was given the job
f looking after the officers' library and was thus
ble to widen his cultural knowledge by reading
Iugo, Zola, Maupassant, Daudet, Pascal, Diderot,
Kropotkin and Bakunin.

A few years later he became friends with Fernand
Senada, with whom he wrote two novels in which
is anarchist views are clearly expressed.

n 1898, when on leave from the army, he met the
ainter Derain in very unusual circumstances. The
rain that was taking them to Paris was derailed
nd so they had to continue the journey on foot,
alking as they went about art and painting. By the
ime they reached Paris they had decided to work
ogether.

n 1901 an exhibition of the works of Van Gogh,
vho had died two years previously, was held at the
Sernheim Gallery. Vlaminck was amazed to see that
'an Gogh had managed to express certain of his
vwn ideas and aspirations about art. Two years later
e exhibited some of his own works at an exhibition

aurice de Vlaminck: Three Women – *wood engraving, 22.2*
17.5 cm – Private Collection, Zurich

organized in the back of Mme Weill's shop by a group of young artists including Matisse. In 1906 the art dealer Ambroise Vollard signed a contract with Vlaminck which enabled the artist to live off the proceeds of his work for the rest of his life. In 1908 he left the Fauves movement and began to make a detailed study of the works of Cézanne. This experience led him, after a brief flirtation with Cubism, to a more mature and controlled form of expression which culminated after the war in a series of paintings with softer colours and dramatically expressive tones.

His life is full of curious episodes. Once when he was in London to paint on the banks of the Thames, he met a young pavement artist drawing the boats on the river. So Vlaminck sat down and started drawing the Moulin Rouge on the paving stones: he managed to earn quite a few shillings from the passers-by!

In 1919 another curious thing happened. He moved to Valmondois near La Nase in the Oise department in Northern France: "I have bought a small house in Valmondois," he wrote, "it is the kind of house I love and often paint in my paintings." Later he learned that Daumier had also lived in the same house and his old housekeeper used to say: "He was a painter, just like you .... He used to work for art galleries, though."

Vlaminck was basically a good man and a fre one, who thought of art and culture as somethin "as natural as yawning when you are tired." H was against artistic "schools" and above al against what he called "boring innovators." H disliked theories about painting and painters an said that "the life of a painter is like the Paris-Bor deaux cycle race. When you get to Tours, yo have to have enough energy left to reach Poitiers In Poitiers you have to find the energy to get to Angoulême and if you are exhausted by the tim you reach Angoulême you might as well not hav started out in the first place. It's all a question o knowing how to distribute your energy properly. He held critics and journalists in low esteem. On journalist, a certain Germain Basin, wrote i 1933: "Vlaminck is a champion of anti-culture believing as he does that every generation has t start from nothing." Vlaminck himself wa famous for his words: "I never go to museums... going to museums debases your personality, jus as talking too much to priests makes you sto believing in God. Science kills one's instincts." Vlaminck's professed dislike of museums wa clearly a deliberate attempt at provocation. I 1923, in a letter to André Salmon, who had at tacked him for his "anti-cultural" ideas, he wrote "I have said and written 'I never go to museums.

Well, my dear Salmon, this is a lie! It's a lie very similar to the one I tell when I say 'I never go to brothels.' Over the last six years or so, a period you know very well, no end of bright young sparks have been filling our heads with their pretentious theories and everyone seems to be turning into mathematicians or metaphysicists overnight. What could I do at a moment like that? How could I answer all those scientific windbags? I would have had to be Poincaré or Flammarion in person to put them in their right place. Sometimes I wanted to shout out or even to laugh, but all I ever said was: 'I don't know how to read or write.' It was easier. Believe me, I have been to museums, just as I have been to brothels. But between you and me, and probably you won't believe me, when I get there I never have the courage to go up-stairs!"

When he was 80 years old, Vlaminck wrote his will: it contains one of the most beautiful passages I have ever read:

This is my last will and testament.

Now I am eighty years old. Life is short. And yet I am amazed that I am still able to look up at the sky and realize that I have managed to survive all the dangers and misfortunes with which our life on earth is fraught. I am amazed that so far I have managed to survive the scientific barbarism of civilized man, amazed that I am not already lying six feet below the ground.

We can touch life with our fingertips. We can see it, hear it and smell it.

I bequeath to everyone, free of duties, the deep emotions, still alive in my old heart, aroused in me by Ruysdael, Brueghel, Courbet, Cézanne, Van Gogh ... and I give away, with no regrets, all that I dislike and reject: pasteurized milk, pharmaceutical products, vitamins, surrogates, and the decorative riddles of abstract art.

Despite my age, I am still able to appreciate good food and to enjoy chicken with mushrooms, steak with potatoes and partridge with cabbage, without mixing up food and pharmaceuticals, the countryside and the sanatorium, work and productivity, love and vice ....

I feel sorry for those who have never known poverty and also for those who never managed to climb out of it by their own strength. Poverty leaves a deep impression. Tears born of love can never be forgotten; they leave a bitter taste in the mouth. When you are hungry and have all your teeth, the taste of dry bread is excellent. If you have a good voice you will sing despite your poverty.

It is not money in its own right that kills artists or writers: but the sense of ease it engenders and the new desires it generates are nasty germs which change the appearance of life, debase inner sentiments and nip fresh flowers in the bud. A work of art is like a seed which sprouts, grows and then blossoms.

Since painters are not inventors, paintings must not be inventions.

Truly personal, original expression is rare. More often than not, artists have to rely on means that have already been used time and again by others. How difficult it is to find your true inner self! How difficult it is to distinguish genuine sentiments from all the others that come rushing to the tip of your brush or pen!

To all young painters I bequeath all the flowers in the fields, the banks of streams, black and white clouds drifting over the land, rivers, woods and trees, hills, roads, villages covered with snow in winter, meadows full of wild flowers, birds and butterflies ....

Shouldn't we try to remember now and then that all these treasures that are reborn with each new season, treasures like the light and the shade or the colour of the sky and the water, are part of a priceless heritage that has inspired countless masterpieces?

They are treasures that belong to everyone and that the taxman cannot touch and which I, an old painter whose fading eyes still remember the sight of fields and meadows and whose ears still recall the sound of the waters rushing down from mountain springs, can bequeath to mankind without having to ask for the services of notaries. Have we enjoyed these treasures enough? Have we admired them enough? Have we fully savoured the emotions of a dawn breaking on a day that soon we shall see no more? Have we managed to transfer all these emotions onto canvas?

I have never asked anybody for anything. Life has given me everything. I have done what I could and I have painted what I saw."

Nude, by Gianni Maimeri

Gianni Maimeri was born on June 21, 1884 in Varano on the banks of the Lake of Comabbio. His father was from the Veneto region of Italy and his mother was French. He received a classical education in Milan and then, in 1903, went to Venice to study art with Giuseppe Alberti. When he returned to Milan in 1906 he joined the "Orologio" group of artists and became friendly with the sculptor Antonio Carminati who was one of the first to appreciate the works of the painter Emilio Gola. The first exhibition of Maimeri's works was held in 1918. He joined the Italian Society of Art but then left after the advent of fascism, preferring to work

one. In 1923 he founded the company Fratelli Maimeri with his brother Carlo, a professional chemist. In 1929 his painting *The End of Winter* won first prize in an art competition organized by the Ministry of Communications. In 1936 one of his paintings, *Snow*, was purchased by the Milan City Council and exhibited in the Milan Art Gallery. His paintings were also purchased by numerous art collectors. His cyclical work *The Thirty Canals of Milan* is now owned by the Ramazzotti family. Paintings in his *Lombard Landscapes* series are part of the collections owned by Galtrucco,

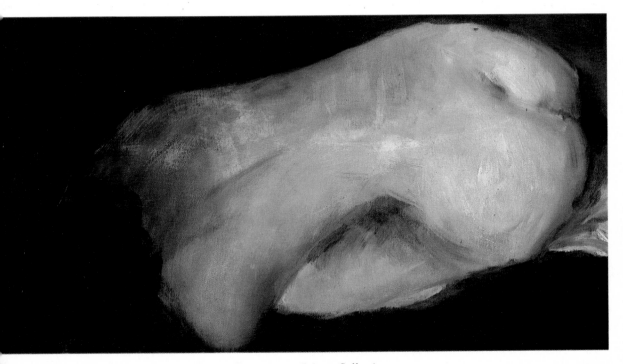

Gianni Maimeri (1884-1951): Nude, ca. 1930 – oil on canvas – Private Collection

Tornaghi and others. Since his death in 1951 critical appraisal of his work has been extremely favourable and his paintings are very highly valued.

In 1930 Mario Sironi wrote: "The most constant feature of Maimeri's painting and the purest is the colour, which is so fine and bright even in the areas of shadow that it brings to mind the use of colour made by certain painters of the Venetian school."

The content of his work lies outside all the controversial research typical of the early 20th century and reflects a lyricism that has its roots in a Lombard tradition that became famous in Europe at the time of Verri and Beccaria.

Gianni Maimeri was one of those painters who saw the rise of the Futurist movement without taking part in it. He felt only scorn for Futurism, as he did for fascism and any form of fanaticism. He took an ironic, disenchanted view of the Italian dictatorship, almost as if he refused to believe what he saw with his own eyes.

At that time there were various forms of reaction against "en plein air" painting, which itself had been a reaction against the classical techniques in vogue before. In Maimeri's times, a painter had to choose whether to remain faithful to the open air school, and hence figurative painting, or whether,

on the other hand, to leave the light behind and paint in the privacy of his studio. Maimeri decided to be a figurative painter, thus choosing isolation, silence, form and colour.

One of Maimeri's main characteristics is the speed with which he worked. The nude we have chosen here is no exception. The small nude figure is drawn with a quick sequence of brush strokes, with the artist working like a sculptor modelling in clay.

The figure seems to have been drawn from memory. Remember that the painter often has only a brief moment in which to capture a person's state of mind by observing their posture and movements. It is important for a painter to have the patience needed for constant observation of his fellow human beings.

The colours Maimeri has used are all yellows and browns: raw sienna, yellow ochre, burnt umber, burnt sienna and Van Dyck brown, plus of course white and a touch of vermilion.

Mortally Wounded, by Gianni Maimeri

Never in my life have I painted a picture merely for the sake of painting a good picture. And I have never started to draw something merely for the sake of drawing a good drawing. For me the most important thing has always been, and still is, to penetrate so deeply into what I am painting that I manage to discover its hidden, innermost aspects. Every cloud, every tree, every landscape and every animal has a hidden secret that is revealed only to those who try to paint it. If you are both profound and a skilful painter you may then find to your amazement that you have painted a really good picture. I have always loved Van Gogh. I find that he manages to catalyze human suffering in a remarkable combination of observation, colour, materials, symbolism, passion and logic.

I find something similar in Munch and in expressionist painting in general.

Once I remember I was in search of a stimulus to help me overcome the academic vision my drawings always seemed to express. I loved drawing then as I do now but I desperately needed to give my work a new emotional charge.

It was about 1968, a period of radical change. I visited an exhibition in Milan of works by the American painter Franz Kline who died in 1962. I was literally speechless when I saw how he used black and white and how his paintings left everything to the subconscious. Like handwriting, the critics said. But anyone who remembers learning how to write, with all those lessons at school and different strokes of the pen, knows that handwriting becomes a subconscious thing only after a great deal of effort. In other words I saw all the rational thought and hard work that must have gone into producing one of Kline's paintings.

The choice of paper was quite casual, but the colour was fundamental: it mattered little if it was a page from the telephone book; black and white suddenly appeared to me to signify the apex of colour and not the absence of it. I tried to interpret this violent vision of painting through figurative subjects. I worked for months to find a new way of expressing myself through my painting.

I painted this particular figure with anger inside me. Effects that could not be achieved with the brush I obtained by scratching the paper with a pencil. I used very big brushes. I didn't want to smooth over anything; I wanted to strike the paper hard. I used my pencil like a hammer. I tore off pieces of newspaper and stuck them on, to give the sensation of torn flesh. Then I put on masses of Ducotone and scratched it with my pencil; made greys by mixing black and white haphazardly. I poured on black so that it looked like blood streaming from a wound. The colours I used were distempers, the type used for painting houses, and maybe also Ducotone. It's all so long ago that I don't remember all the details. The whole thing was done on rough wrapping paper. The newspaper, torn slowly by hand, was stuck on with vinavil dilted with water (3 parts of paste to 6 parts of water). After sticking the paper on, I went over the whole thing again with the brush using heavily diluted colours. Then I put on the white and the grey (which I had obtained by roughly mixing black and white). I painted with a flat, no. 30 brush. I remember that period very well. I painted furiously, almost attacking my pictures. This is a phase that all painters should go through in order to become "virtuosos" in the use of painting materials.

The Palette Knife

The palette knife has always been used in painting. It was not until Courbet, however, that it came to be thought of as one of the artist's most expressive tools.

The special relationship the painter has with his palette knife is similar to the relationship between the sculptor and his clay. The paint becomes a material, to be laid on as you wish – thickly, streakily, lumpily and, at all times, synthetically.

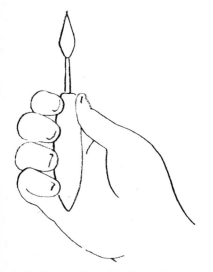

Luisella Lissoni: Seated Nude – *oil on canvas*

Using the palette knife is not a technique that allows you to express detail; it forces you to adopt a synthetic view of your subject.

The seated nude shown here, painted by Luisella, is a good example of this. While she was painting, I stopped to watch her on several occasions. She was not her usual self.

Her delicate method of painting, part of her own character, had been replaced by a more aggressive, almost violent, approach.

The more I watched her, the more she seemed like one of the three musketeers engaged in a furious sword fight.

When she packed up work for the day, the paint scattered about on the floor bore witness to the struggle that had taken place between Luisella and her canvas. This type of painting encourages you to paint in an aggressive way.

Look carefully at paintings done with a palette knife and you will see clearly what I mean.

Let's now take a look at different kinds of palette knives and how they are used. There are various types of palette knives. The effect they create depends partly on the shape of the blade. Most painters choose one or two shapes according to the effects they want.

Palette knives are not easy to use.

They must be held in such a way as to prevent their slipping along the canvas when painting. Remember that the palette knife was originally designed for mixing the paints and not for actual painting. It is therefore the painter who has to adapt to the tool and not vice versa.

Either the flat part of the blade or the tip can be used to apply the paint, depending on the effect required. As you use the knife, you will soon learn how to achieve different effects and you will gradually discover the details of the technique.

Never be afraid; use the palette knife boldly. Beginners are often frightened of the palette knife and tend to use only the tip. This is because of an unconscious desire to use it like a brush.

As you paint, observe the position of your wrist. It must be a continuation of the palette knife and

Hand-forged steel palette knives in various sizes, with wooden handles and brass ferrules

110

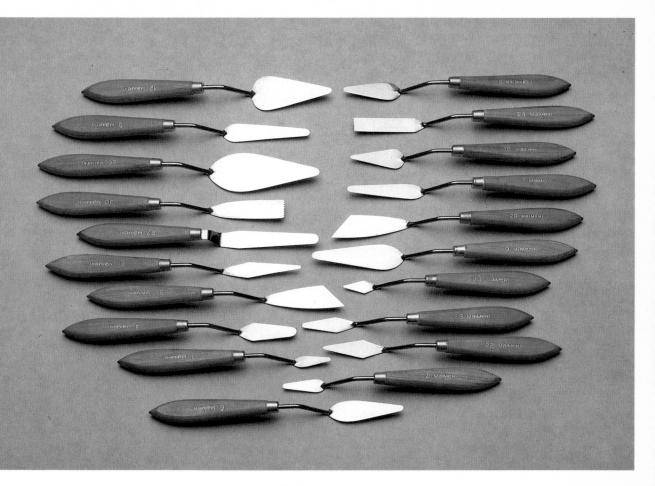

your hand, in line with the arm. This, of course, is when the canvas is resting on an easel; if the canvas is on a worktop, it is a different matter.

I personally enjoy working with a palette knife, especially when painting large pictures. It forces you to look for new ways of expressing yourself through your paints and is therefore used to its best effect in abstract or expressionist painting.

From the Figurative to the Abstract: Franz Kline

Franz Kline was born in Pennsylvania on May 23, 1910. His father, of German origin, was the owner of a bar. His mother had emigrated to the United States when she was seventeen. In 1917 his father committed suicide for reasons which the newspapers of the time described as financial difficulties.

On March 21, 1919 Franz Kline was sent to an orphanage, where he studied English, arithmetic and mechanics. In the meantime his mother remarried and so Franz eventually went back to his new family which had settled in the town of Leighton.

From 1927 to 1931 he attended high school and then, while convalescing after an accident to his knee, he decided to enroll in an art school to become a cartoonist. In the same year he began to attend Boston University. Two years later he met an art student called Martha Kinney who became his constant companion and model. In 1935 he left the USA for England and during the journey he met Frank Hahn.

The period that followed was an extremely good one for Kline. In London he visited museums and art galleries and also attended the Heatherley School of Fine Art.

In January 1937 he met his future wife Elisabeth, a ballet dancer. She posed for him and also introduced him to the world of classical music and ballet.

In 1938 he returned to the States and settled in New York. Elisabeth followed him shortly afterwards and they were married by the end of the year. During the same year, on his birthday, he went to see a performance of one of Wagner's operas. Wagner's music was to have a profound effect on his future painting. In 1939 he also met the two men who were to become his most important patrons during his figurative period, Theodore J. Edlich and David Orr.

Kline and his wife were evicted from their lodgings several times but finally settled at 43 Hudson Street. In 1942 one of his paintings entitled *The Artist's Wife* was included in the annual

xhibition of the National Academy of Design. In
943 he won the S.J. Wallace prize with the paint-
ng *Palmerton Pa*. During the 1940s he was a
requent visitor to the Cedar Bar in New York, a
vell-known meeting place for artists. He also met
Charles Egan who decided to organize an exhibi-
ion of his works.

n 1951 the Ninth Street Show took place and
Kline's paintings were exhibited alongside those
f Albers, de Kooning, Gorky, Motherwell and
'ollock. In 1953 the house he was living in was
narked off for demolition and he was evicted for
he umpteenth time. In March 1954 he was a
nember of the organizing committee of the con-
ress entitled "Abstract Art Around The World
'oday." During this period he added brown to his
wo basic colours black and white. He also used
olour in small works such as *Red, Yellow, Green
nd Blue*.

n 1957 he finally found a permanent studio where
e was able to work for the rest of his days without
ear of eviction. "My studio is magnificent," he
vrote to his friends, "very large and spacious." In
960 he designed a huge back-cloth for a ballet
vhich was the largest work he ever produced. In
he same year he travelled around Europe and
pent a long time in Italy, visiting Venice (where
ne of his works had been exhibited in 1956

Franz Kline (1910-1962): Small Seated Figure, *1947 –
ink and pastel on paper, 12.7 × 11.4 cm*

113

during the "Biennale"), Milan, Vicenza and Florence. When he returned to New York he was taken to hospital for a series of check-ups and heart disease was diagnosed. He died on May 13, 1962.

I first went to an exhibition of Kline's work in 1968. It impressed me deeply in a way that was new to me. Looking at his paintings I experienced a sense of suffering that was almost physical. I felt that behind those black masses on his canvases there lay the structural solidity of a large medieval fresco. The paintings were magnificently unnerving. I decided to find out more. I discovered that unlike many of his American contemporaries Kline had passed through a "figurative" period and that the paintings he had done during these figurative years had been highly successful. More recently I read an essay on the life of Kline: from it he emerges as a deep, penetrating personality and a very unhappy man. I have always admired artists who manage to remain warm-hearted despite their skill and fame. I like reading Vasari's lives of famous painters since he fills his pages with interesting anecdotes about the artists' personal lives. We learn about the altruism of Masaccio or about how Cimabue taught Giotto many of the secrets of his art. I mention all this because when I read about Kline's

life I felt that I was reading about a generous warm-hearted person like those so ably described by Vasari.

People who knew Kline well often describe the carefree, friendly side of his character, pointing out that he also had a sharp and often bitter way of poking fun at himself. This happy-go-lucky, altruistic image of Kline – who often used to say that what counted most in art was knowing how to give to others – is in contrast with the solitary, pessimistic side of a man whose father had committed suicide and whose mother had suffered for

1

114

many years from a mental illness. Kline, however, never let these dramatic events get the better of him and he never let despair show through in his art. He was never taciturn or mysterious.

The story of his "conversion" to abstract art is well-known. One day he saw a magnified, upside-down sketch of a rocking chair projected onto a wall. His amazement when he saw the self-sufficiency of the marks his brush had made on the canvas led him to make radical changes to his style of painting. He did not, however, make a complete break with his past and his years of academic training. He simply managed to keep tradition at a logical distance and to concentrate more on the emotional and formal stimuli of the outside world.

Now let's examine one of Kline's last paintings, entitled *Tragedy* (on page 116). The painting is dated 1961, the year before his death. At that time he was suffering from severe rheumatic fever which affected his heart, giving him great pain as well as deliriously high temperatures. The painting does in fact look like a delirious dream, with its great patches of electric blue on top of the yellow background. The yellow of the background is not all the same: yellow ochre alternates with cadmium yellow. The colours interweave to form a kind of carpet on which the other colours, painted on with a large, hard brush, appear to be lying. The blue, vermilion and dark cadmium red give an impression of vertical and horizontal inclination, creating a sense of drama which brings to mind the limitless tragedy of Goya. An abstract painting is never the result of pure chance: it is the sum of its colours, vibrations, dynamics, movement and harmony. In many figurative

2

Franz Kline: Rocking Chair, *1948 –*
ink on paper, 12.7 × 10.2 cm –
sketch seen the right way up (1) and upside-down (2)

Franz Kline: Tragedy, *1961 – oil on board, 76.2 × 101.6 cm – Private Collection*

ketches and drawings it is easy to find small esigns or marks that are identical to those ainted by Kline. Is it perhaps because of these etails that the whole painting comes to life? If nis is so, then it is possible that they create the ame effect in a non-figurative painting. Is all this oo complicated? Not really. Try magnifying a etail from a painting by Goya. If you look at it n isolation, you will have the feeling that you are ooking at an abstract painting.

How to Move from Figurative Painting to Abstract Painting

t is extremely difficult in just a few pages to peak about the slow transition from figurative ainting to abstract painting that took up some wenty-nine years of my life and work. xplaining the reasons from a theoretical point of iew is quite easy; the difficult part is all that lies ehind this: the choice of certain colours rather han others, the decision to spread the colours in certain way and so on. hese are decisions that come from emotional xperiences and are therefore difficult to put into ew words. n my opinion, abstract painting is first and foremost a matter of construction. Instinct alone means nothing. Instinct is in any case the result of subconscious reasoning. Let me explain what I mean. If we have to jump over a ditch or a stream we know immediately whether we are able to clear it just by looking at it, and we also know how much thrust is needed and how to position our legs and feet.

All these instinctive mechanisms are the result of long experience built up day by day from early childhood, experimenting with movements and their results first under our mother's protection

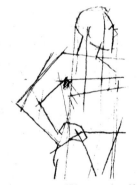

and then on our own. We methodically build up our experience and memorize it.

It is a bit like a spider weaving its web. To us all the webs look the same but in fact they are all very different from one another. Each web has to be

117

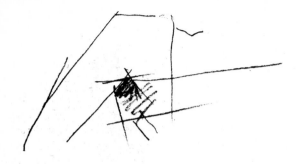

examples may not seem to have much in common with painting, the comparison is valid and good. When I started to draw at art school I had a very good teacher. He insisted that we learn to draw in the traditional way, i.e. by drawing all the vertical and horizontal lines that have always made up the basic architecture of a figure. My journey towards abstract art began there.

If we examine together the construction lines of a human figure it may help you to understand why I say this. You will notice some straight lines that are confidently drawn. These represent the external structure and the internal points where the bones and muscles meet.

Look carefully at the structure of the point where the chest meets the armpit. This part is shaded in the sketch. In synthesis, what we have is a triangle, or rather part of what could be a triangle, a rectangle or a square.

adapted to suit the surrounding environment, such as the distance between two branches of a tree, the distance from the nearest corner and so on. The final result is always a geometrical figure resembling the previous one, since the spider's experience of constructing webs is so great that he will never make a mistake. Although these

So, we may ask ourselves, what use is knowing how to draw perfectly when then we find from an analysis of a part of our drawing that all it involves is the top of a triangle? The answer is that it is a lot of use. It helps us learn how to construct our drawings in a dynamic way.

So now you have learned to jump the first ditch, so to speak, with the helping hand of a friend. Now you know where to start from and where you want

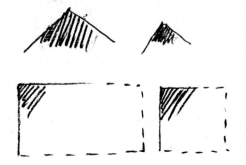

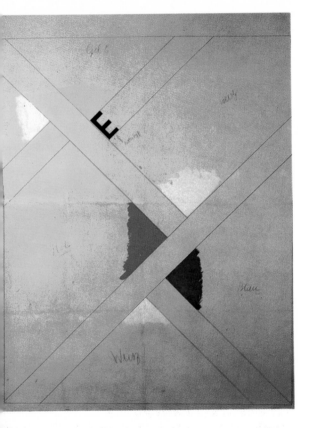

Theo van Doesburg (1883-1931): Project for a Poster, *1924 – mixed technique, 150 × 115.5 cm – Private Collection, Milan*

Vladimir Tatlin (1885-1953): Project for a Counter Relief, *1916 – Indian ink, 27 × 19.5 cm – Czwiklitzer, Baden-Baden*

119

to get to. Look at the examples on the preceding page: the first is part of a project for a poster by Theo van Doesburg and the second is an Indian ink sketch by Vladimir Tatlin. Can you see how far our original sketch of an armpit has come?

Abstract Art

Now we are going to take a few more steps in the direction of abstract art. It is obvious that the reasons why a painter decides to paint in the abstract are different from those that determine the choice of figurative painting.

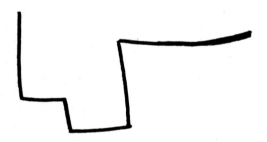

The most important thing is to learn how to capture certain feelings and how to keep them alive in your memory. To help you understand what I mean I am going to invent a situation. The situation is

deliberately simple and linear but it should serve to explain the long process which leads an artist to recreate certain emotions in a certain way.

I will tell the story in the first person, using one of my own paintings to explain the various stages. I am out shopping for certain objects I need in order to set up some still life studies for my pupils

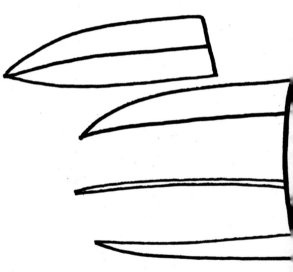

to copy. I am wandering through the town somewhat aimlessly and suddenly the street I am walking along bends slightly to the left into a wider street and then winds off again to the right

start walking in that direction when I see a bare wall, yellow and pink in colour. Here we have the first memories and sensations which have to be put onto my canvas. The pattern is: the street, the wall, the colours. As I go on I see a stuffed bird in a shop window, a raven, and I notice its beak and its glass eyes. I remember that the raven is a symbol of time, of solitude, of filial love (in Japan) and of perspicacity (*Genesis*, 8, verses 6-7). It symbolizes many contradictory things: sometimes it is the bird of darkness and death and at other times it stands for love and protection. The raven is black, and black is the colour of the start of life, associated with germination and fertilization. Then, depending on whether the black is opaque or glossy, it can become the apex of colour, the negation of colour or its synthesis. It is the colour of the damned and also the colour of those who renounce all their worldly goods. In the West it is the colour of mourning, though in Ancient Egypt or in Africa it becomes a symbol of fertility. White, its opposite, lies at both ends of the chromatic scale. Pure white can be the negation of colour or colour 'par excellence.' It is the colour of transition in rites involving the transition from life to death and then rebirth. It also reminds me of winter. The white of snow. The yellow of ears of corn. Ravens and crows eating the corn and carrying it away ... I remember Poe's poem about ravens ... I remember the cornfield and the crows painted by Van Gogh. And then the white of the sun, the sky getting bluer in the evenings, the stove and the warmth emanating from it ... the red of the fire. All these symbols and all these colours descend upon the canvas and bring about transformations. My analysis shows how all the colours intermingle. But we still have not finished. The wings of the raven as it discovers the freedom of flight remind me of the hair and body of a distant loved one ... Ultramarine blue mixed with titanium white, and then watered down cerulean blue ... so transparent that it is hardly distinguishable from the white of the canvas. A nude painted by Degas ...

The important thing is to arouse emotions. Anyone looking at the painting must be carried away by the feelings it arouses. All the different elements must make up a composition or a story as they do in a painting by Bosch, one of the triptychs, for example. The rhythm of the story can vary, however. The white part must take up one third of the painting, while the grey at the top is wider and the darker third is larger again. The symbols are superimposed during the charcoal sketch. Then changes are made until all the elements harmonize with one another like musical

notes. The colours must be well balanced; the white part moves into the foreground, the dark patches move to the sides or to the top. At the top on the right a white light becomes an escape route. This optical effect is the result of the grey and black outlines which create the sensation of an interior and an exterior. The painting is now finished. Obviously this is not the only route taken by artists when they construct their pictures. Every painter develops his own methods according to his cultural and emotional experiences. Ever since 1970 I have followed the methods used by the Russian Suprematists since I felt that their ways of constructing their paintings were very similar to mine. But there are of course many other ways.

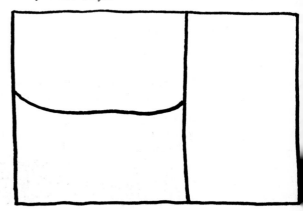

Lying Nude, by Nicolas de Staël

When a painter ceases to be an amateur and becomes deeply involved in his work, it is as if he were under the influence of a magic spell. All his thoughts are directed at his work. He lives to paint; never the other way round.

Every single object, every person and every slight change in the light is seen as a function of his art. He often paints in his dreams. He paints with his thoughts as well as with his hands. Thousands of different pictures come into his head every hour of every day and yet he can paint only about one every month.

A good painter paints by themes. The themes are arranged into cycles. At the end of each cycle which may last months or even years, the artist feels exhausted and depressed. Sometimes this period coincides with a moment of difficulty and this can cause a feeling of loneliness and even suicidal thoughts. There are many famous examples: Pellizza da Volpedo, Van Gogh, de Staël and many others. Some never find the courage to actually put an end to their lives and try to drown their sorrows with alcohol, as did Toulouse-Lautrec, Courbet and lots more.

The best way to survive such periods is to go on painting and drawing, to return to figurative sub-

Nicolas de Staël (1914-1955): Lying Nude – *charcoal on paper, 106 × 149 cm – Private Collection, Zurich*

124

ects such as still life, vases of flowers or objects reflected in the water. This perhaps explains why painters like Picasso and Mondrian returned to figurative painting. The return may be short-lived or may last a long time, depending on how much energy had been used up previously.

De Staël's figurative period must have been the result of a crisis of this type.

Artists who paint figuratively know that theirs is not necessarily a backward step. It is only a backward step if an artist paints in this way merely to follow the official trends of the market or to make critics or art collectors happy.

If we look at de Staël's charcoal figures, we will realize that such expressive force can only be achieved after a long experience of abstract painting. In abstract art, the materials themselves take the place of perspective and tonal expression. In de Staël's drawings, charcoal, used mostly by classical artists, gives a slightly blurred effect and seems to have been used almost like a digging tool.

The figure is divided into two quite separate parts – light and shade – and halftones are eliminated. The figure is really only the sensation of a figure, as if the painter were looking at her through steamed-up glasses.

Extremely interesting in this respect are the re-

1

marks made by E.H. Gombrich in *Freud and the Psychology of Art*:

"I'm sorry but I am going to ask you to look at another example of *art officiel*; this one is a real eyesore, Bonnencontre's *Three Muses* (1). I'll spare you an analysis of what makes it so awful.

125

2

3

But let's see whether we can make this sickly sweet mixture a little better by adding something more appetizing. Look at the photograph of the same painting as seen through a sheet of corrugated glass (2). You have to agree that it has improved a lot. We have to work harder to reconstruct the picture and are therefore less put off by

it. The second photograph (3) shows the sam painting seen through the same sheet of glase held further away from the painting itself. Now deserves to be called 'interesting.' The effort w have to make to put the parts back together give added strength to the picture and makes it quit 'appetizing.' Really I should have patented th invention of mine because I'm sure it has great economic potential. In future, when you find a painting of *Innocence in Peril* or a stag called *The King of the Forest* in your attic, you will no longer have to throw it away or give it to one of your maids. Just cover it with a sheet of corrugated glass and you'll have a good painting!" Gombrich's remarks are extraordinarily revealing.

Cézanne also paints as if he were looking at the figures through a pane of corrugated glass. Or rather our mind has to become a pane of glass in order to filter the picture and interpret it. All this is the result of great effort and continuous practice. This may seem impossible to a young artist copying a sleeping cat or a vase of flowers. But try seeing what happens when you give a confident, bold, sharp, sweeping stroke with an interior decorator's brush – it's an intense visual emotion. An emotion as intense as the one which guided your arm in the first place.

But let's return to de Staël's drawing of a nude. This is not a gentle nude pleasantly resting; it is a woman full of human suffering who is having to sit for a tormented artist in search of his own inner peace. Look at the black parts which blend into half-tones only momentarily at the point where the pencil leaves the paper. Only an artist with a good classical knowledge of the human figure could achieve such synthesis and such force. It is important to study the work of abstract painters and thus learn how to appreciate and evaluate this kind of artistic expression.

Moving on to the second figure, which is even more synthetic and dramatic, you will notice that there are no arms, no legs and no feet. The head is just a black mark with a hint of lighting on what we assume to be the cheek. And yet we feel the presence of a human figure and also a sense of drama. The figure is as powerful and solid as an Egyptian statue. If we look closely we will find many similarities with Mondrian's figures shown on pages 71-73. This of course does not mean that de Staël took his inspiration from Mondrian; it merely highlights a natural phase in the transition from figurative to abstract art.

To achieve an effect such as this, it is necessary to use wide designer's charcoals and not the usual thin ones. These pencils enable you to draw thin lines and wide ones and force you to use the technique of synthesis.

To achieve the synthesis of an arm using a wide charcoal pencil, hold it so that it presses more at one end than at the other. The line drawn will then be blurred and yet natural.

Remember that charcoal is not suitable for all types of drawing. It can crumble as you use it or

reak as you are drawing important lines. Nevertheless it is an essential tool that all artists must learn to use. Practise on rough paper such as wrapping paper, pouncing paper or special paper designed for charcoal drawings. With charcoal it is possibl e to obtain delicate or violent effects as required. The discovery of Suprematism was a revelation for me. It happened between the years 965 and 1970. My first reaction was to reject it, but then my curiosity got the better of me. "Malevich put everything into a square pot and boiled it up to zero point": that's what I used to think about his paintings. His black squares on white backgrounds had completely overturned my ideas about beauty and had sent me emotionally back to square one. In order to go where the wings of the raven were taking me, this was where I had to start. I remembered Malevich's painting *Woman with a Rake* and above all, the head. Half white and half black. Light and shade. Day and night. Being and not being. The female figure in

the first study (which we have already seen in the first picture) had somehow to evolve. I had to make the egg, as it were. I had to study a perfectly oval face, a face with enough feeling behind it to support the allegory needed to build up a feeling of depth. Malevich once wrote:
"Cézanne's art is one of the greatest breakthroughs in the whole history of art because it reveals what I call pictorial feeling in all its purity. Cézanne marks one peak in the development of the history of painting. There is a self portrait by Cézanne that is remarkable for the way in which pictorial feeling is defined. Anatomically, however, the portrait does not correspond to reality. It cannot therefore truthfully be called a self portrait.
The model and the way it is represented are differ-

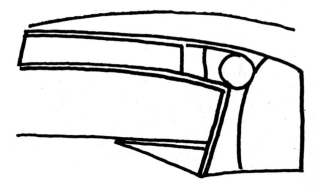

ent; all that remains is the character and some of the facial features. There is an even greater difference as far as the colours are concerned. The face is covered with a layer of colour that could in no way be thought of as corresponding to reality. We are, then, looking at a painting which resembles neither the shape nor the colour of the model. From this, however, we must not conclude that Cézanne was a bad painter because what we are looking at is a reflection of the feeling of 'real' painting or, in other words, a reflection of a value more important and more precious than the 'real' model. In the self portrait, then, there are many changes with respect to the model. This means that the representation of the model is no longer 'real'. Even the colours are not 'real'. Followers of Cézanne find in nature the same conditions as the Impressionists found in the representation of colour. In the same way Cézanne and his followers consider objects as conditions (but not forms) of the reflection of pictorial feeling. For Cézanne, as for the Impressionists, the actual shape of the object is not important since he is a painter.

Consequently in neither case are objects considered as the forms of the reflection. We therefore arrive at the conclusion that all the forms that we regard as forms – still life, human figures – are not the same forms as the forms of the reflection; just as in music the form of the musical instrument is not the form of the music and in literature the form of the letters is not the form of the poem. After Cézanne the line of pictorial reflection led to the total deformation of the object, where all the pictorial elements are reformed according to the depth of the pictorial feeling. It is at this point that a new pictorial medium, one that no longer creates forms, makes its appearance. The more expressive the pictorial feeling, the stabler the imagination of the painter and the quicker the arrival of the moment when the details of the objects disappear completely. What we used to regard as form thus exists no longer. And so what is left for us to perceive? For Cézanne the answer is the artistic elements; for Matisse, the colour; for the Cubists, the contrasts."

At this point I needed something to trigger off the construction of my new painting.

Like painters in past times I was looking for the right image and the right elements to set me off constructing my painting since, however abstract it may turn out to be, a painting needs to be based on experience if it is to be more than just decorative.

Many years earlier, the book *Zoo or Non-Love Letters* by Sklovsky had fascinated me, especially "Letter Six":

"You gave me two jobs.
1) Not to telephone you.
2) Not to see you.
Now I am a busy man.
But there is a third job: not to think about you.
You didn't give me that one."

These elements are sufficient to give life to a painting. If the painter is lucky (or unlucky) enough to actually experience such a sitation, the picture will be full of feeling, suffering and life. But let's return to the subject of how the picture starts its life on the canvas. First, the painter takes the figurative elements, such as the ideal female face. The egg as a symbol. The egg/face is divided into three parts: light and dark, happiness and unhappiness.

The Symbol of the Egg

The egg is regarded as the container of life, the home of the embryo. The idea that the beginning of the world is somehow linked to the egg is shared by Celts, Greeks, Egyptians, Phoenicians, Canadians, Tibetans, Chinese and Hindus. The egg is in fact a primordial element containing all the different aspects of human existence in embryo form.

Even more common is the idea of the cosmic egg, laid in primordial waters and hatched, according to the Indian legend, by the goose Hamsa. The egg then split in two to create heaven and earth.

For some Inca peoples the cosmic egg is a representation of one of the highest of all Gods.

The egg is also a symbol of rebirth, the renewal of nature or the return to life.

Other symbols include the home, the nest and the mother's womb, from which the "chick", half-free

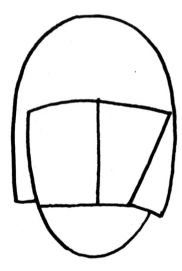

and half-enclosed, wishes to escape, despite the protection and security it offers. Like the symbol of the mother, the egg is also the symbol of the inner conflict between what we are and what we seem, between introversion and extroversion.

The third part, the chin, is the point where the hand rests as if to hold back thoughts. When we are deep in thought we often rest our chin on our hands. The cut of the hair, moving on a horizontal line, can change into a synthesis of one wing of a raven seen in close-up.

The other wing, seen vertically in the background, gives a sense of perspective which leads towards the depth of night, the time when sufferers from insomnia lie awake or, in other words, the depths of the soul. The figure now needs to be given an enigmatic air. Like one of Michelangelo's poses. One shoulder in the foreground and one turning away like a figure whose face turns towards you for one fleeting moment and yet whose body still indicates its intention to go away. The moment before saying goodbye.

This in itself would be extremely static, but if there is a sign of movement on the left-hand side the figure will appear to be moving. The raven in the foreground protects the whole composition by holding it in place.

Colour must now find its place in the composition we have patiently constructed. The colours of the night which slowly change into the colours of the dawn. The colours of peach blossom taking on new hues as we move from right to left, from grey-blue to violet-blue, pink and the pale pink of the flowers in full light. The greenish glow of dawn and the yellow of the sun we hope is about to rise.

And that's it. One possible explanation of a picture deliberately painted in a figurative manner in order to help you enter a world that even some so-called experts find difficult to accept.

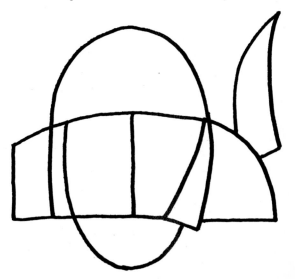

Before We Continue Our Journey towards Abstract Art

Nicolas de Staël took his own life on March 16, 1955.

De Staël was born on January 5, 1914 in St. Petersburg. His father was a major general in the army and his mother, a rich, well-educated woman, was a lover of painting and music and it was she who encouraged her son to take up painting.

After the Russian Revolution the family emigrated to Poland. In 1921 his father died and in 1922, his mother. One of his mother's friends took charge of Nicolas and his sisters, taking them to Brussels where a certain Mr Fricero became their guardian.

After attending a Jesuit school, Nicolas enrolled in the Royal Academy of Fine Arts in Brussels in 1933. Here he won a prize with a painting entitled *Un bateau fantôme*. After this he travelled to Holland and then to Paris, where he was greatly impressed by the works of Cézanne, Braque and Matisse. He spent one year in Spain and then travelled around Italy. In 1935 he returned to Brussels and worked for the International Exhibition held that year. Then he made an important journey to Morocco where he painted many pictures from real life. He met the painter Jeanine Teslar who became his constant companion until her death in 1946. At first the couple lived together in complete poverty in a small studio in Paris. When war broke out in 1939 de Staël joined the Foreign Legion and fought in Tunisia. In 1940 he moved to Nice. Here he met other painters, intellectuals, extremists and surrealists. He began to isolate himself from the world but at the same time he finally found his own personal style of painting.

In 1942 his daughter Anna was born and de Staël returned to Paris. In spite of extreme difficulty – the family was penniless, and winter in the big city was extremely cold – de Staël's best work was started during this period.

He painted very large works, using any kind of canvas he could get his hands on, working day and night. Starting from a realistic form of expression, he moved gradually through various stages to a far freer style of painting.

It should be remembered that at that time there were very few "abstract" paintings hanging on the

Nicolas de Staël: Lying Nude, *1954 – oil on canvas, 97 × 145 cm – Private Collection*

walls of art galleries. The general public was unable to appreciate such paintings since they saw them as just a lot of strange shapes and colours. Occasionally de Staël received visits from people interested in his paintings. Every now and then he even managed to sell one or two. Yet he hated talking about his art.

In 1944 he met Braque, a man he greatly admired, and soon they became great friends. In April of the same year a small gallery ran the risk of or-

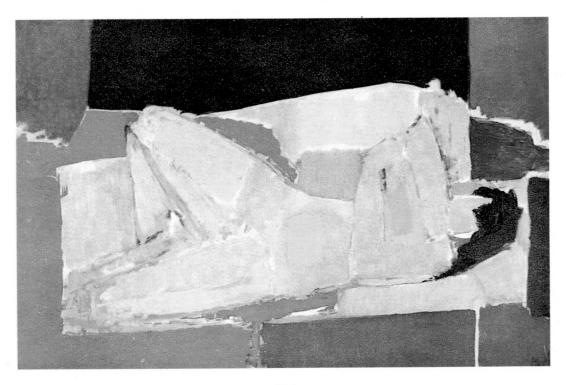

ganizing an exhibition of works by de Staël, Kandinsky, Doméla and Magnelli under the title of "Abstract Paintings." A few months later the same gallery held another exhibition devoted entirely to de Staël.

In February 1945 another exhibition of his works was held at the Jeanne Bucher gallery. It was extremely well attended and there was talk of de Staël as a "revelation." In the summer of that year the family had to move to a tiny attic apartment since they were evicted from their previous home. Life was extremely difficult and de Staël went on painting very large pictures.

Things went from bad to worse. Evicted again, the family found an even darker and colder room to live in. De Staël's paintings, however, were beginning to be noticed, especially by the collector Jean Bauret who had also become a close friend.

The death of Jeanine in 1946 came as a tremendous blow to de Staël. Painting became the only reason for his existence. Finally in 1947 he was able to move to a larger studio and was lucky enough to meet the art dealer Théodore Schempp who introduced his work to the American public.

In 1948 de Staël married Françoise Chapouton. In the same year he became friendly with Jacques Dubourg who did much to get his paintings known and also acted as his dealer.

His works were by now being exhibited all over the world: Montevideo, New York, London, Paris. In 1953 de Staël visited New York and then travelled in Italy. In 1954 he found a studio in Antibes in France, right next to the sea. He worked very hard. When he stopped painting, he would begin to draw. He drew large nudes and landscapes. He started another very large canvas which was to remain unfinished. He committed suicide during the night of March 16, 1955.

I consider Nicolas de Staël to be a very great painter. I have always admired him for the fact that he never lost sight of figurative art. His was a synthetic form of figurative art, achieved through his excursions into abstract art and back again. I have never been fond of purely abstract painters who reject figurative expression completely.

I prefer painters who move about from the figurative to the abstract like the liquid in a communicating vessel. The one experience completes and enhances the other. The two things must become one, as they do in any painter who knows the importance of research.

Nicolas de Staël had to struggle continuously against poverty and hunger. The same kind of truggle that Millet, Daumier, Van Gogh and Kline had to fight. Hardship, fatigue, suffering and anguish. Hours and hours in a freezing cold tudio with no money to pay the heating bills, with he nervous tension of artistic creation hiding the eed to sleep and to eat. Paintings created in this vay are always full of intense feeling.

n de Staël's paintings we can see the fury that vent into their creation, the hours of work by day and by night, with no money to buy even a proper anvas.

et's look at the nude de Staël painted in 1954. It s clear how the experience of abstract art has enhanced his chromatic and structural skills. The hythm set up by the full and empty spaces, such as the wall and the floor and the areas of light and hade, are pretexts for creating synthetized suraces with subdued colours that always create a oreground, a fugue and a background. The sofa or chair the woman is resting on is a continuation of the figure. It is painted in exactly the same colours and only the reds, blues and pale violets separate the two forms. The figure is curled up, covering her mouth and her breasts. Her legs are bent. The shape of the body can only just be made out and yet it is as powerful, violent and exciting as a tornado.

Casorati's Nudes

Nudes play an important role in Casorati's painting. They are drawn with elementary, categorical shapes, as one would draw soup-bowls, eggs or books. The lines are ellipsoidal and the colours uniform, two features which recur constantly in Casorati's works. Most of Casorati's paintings are female nudes. During the 1930s the critics were annoyed by these nude figures: the poses seemed to be too rigid and anonymous and the figures had a dismayed, lost look about them, the antithesis of beauty or charm.

Casorati painted his nudes inside his studio (as we can see from the easels and picture frames, the floor covered with pieces of paper, plaster statues and mirrors), and at the same time he reminds us of the historical traditions of Italian art.

In 1920 the "Biennale" in Venice played host to an exhibition of the works of Cézanne. This was an unforgettable occasion for all artists of the period and Casorati was no exception. In those post-war years he was still suffering the aftereffects of the drama of his father's suicide, and his paintings, such as the large *Woman Waiting*, were severe expressions of great solitude.

His compositions often consisted of a nude model and a second form or object, such as a cupboard,

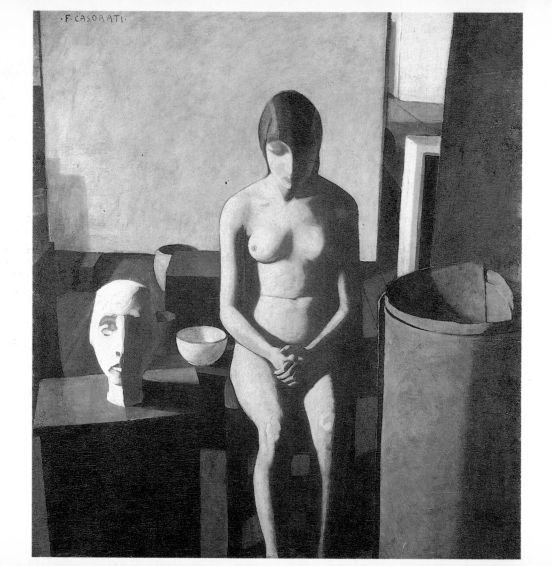

Felice Casorati: Woman and Armour,
*1921 – tempera on canvas,
48.5 × 144 cm –
Civic Museum of
Modern Art, Turin*

*On the left: Felice Casorati (1886-
1963):* Nude Girl (Girl with Linoleum), *1921 –
tempera on plywood board, 112 × 100 cm –
Private Collection*

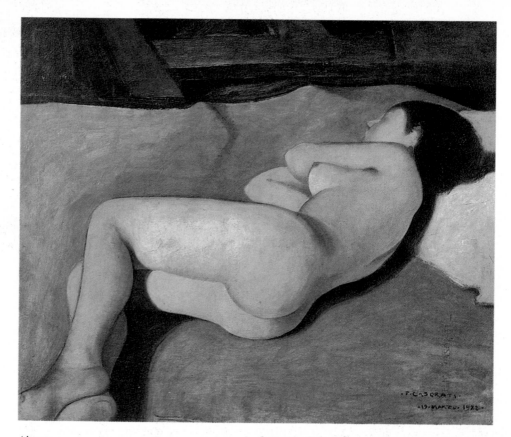

Above:
Felice Casorati: Study for Noontide, *1922 –*
oil on cardboard, 60 × 70 cm –
Regional Collection, Florence

Opposite: Felice Casorati: Noontide, *1923 –*
oil on board, 120 × 130 cm –
Revoltella Museum – Gallery of Modern Art,
Trieste

a roll of linoleum or a plaster statue. The opposition suggested a kind of conflict between art and nature.

With *Noontide* in 1923 his compositions became more complex, with the perspective clearly indicating the column on the right-hand side of the picture as the focal point. The three nudes revolve around this hub like spokes in a wheel. Alongside the nudes, which are painted in a monotone, we find the two red slippers, the black hat and the shiny surface of the vase. In the background we no longer find square frames but white drapery which creates warmer and unusually gentle shadows. The naturalness of the whole scene is impressive. With *Platonic Conversation* (1925), we have a more tangible vision of female beauty, with a very beautiful woman lying in a pose reminiscent of Titian's Venus. The interested observer of such sensuous, innocent beauty is set apart. The painting forms part of an artistic tradition which ranges from Giorgione to the *Olympia* of Manet.

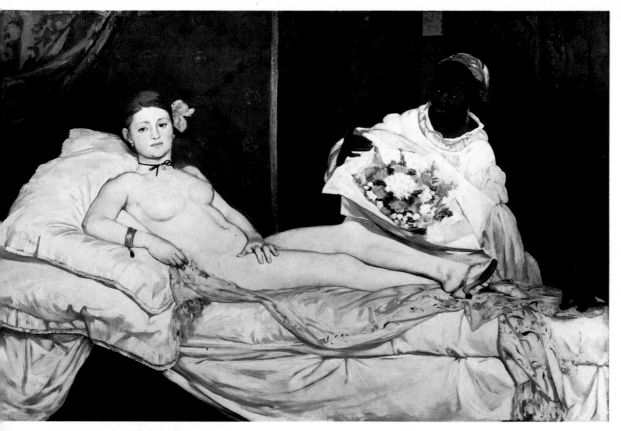

Edouard Manet: Olympia, *1863 –*
oil on canvas, 130 × 190 cm –
Musée d'Orsay, Paris

Casorati's Nudes from the Point of View of Technique

Technically speaking, Casorati's nudes belong to the painting of the Renaissance. His apparently basic technique is based on a profound knowledge of human anatomy. The period in which Casorati lived and worked abounds with artists I personally think of as raving lunatics. For me, the early years of Futurism were characterized by a series of mad, political gestures which have nothing to do with art. Casorati stood aloof from all this. He went on working alone in his studio pursuing an idea that was light years away from the vision of the artist being so rhetorically championed at that time. His line drawings are as solid as stone pillars. So

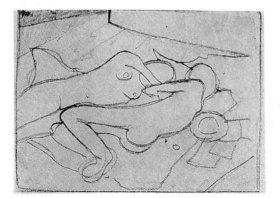

let's try to draw as Casorati did. Studying a painter in this way does not necessarily mean imitating him. All the great painters probably wanted to learn to draw like their illustrious predecessors. Toulouse-Lautrec would have liked to draw like Degas, Degas like Ingres, Ingres like Raphael, Raphael like Leonardo and so on.
They all studied their predecessors not to copy them slavishly but to attempt to understand and perhaps rival their skills and technique.
The first thing to understand about Casorati's painting is the importance of the lines and hence the drawing. This is the secret of his art, as it was for Degas or for Ingres. The sequence shown here starts from the first rough sketch. A picture is born in the mind of the artist. The model must have a body like that of the figure in the artist's head. During the posing sessions the artist will therefore make the model take up lots of different poses until he finds the one which corresponds to his idea. One important exercise in this respect is practising sketching figures from memory. Another basic rule is to draw the sketch with continuous lines, eliminating all unnecessary details. The image must be "frozen" onto the sheet of paper. Generally speaking, very soft pencils are used, though a skilled painter may use a fountain pen or a felt-tipped pen. The sketch (which I find

omes as a kind of mental release) can have great rtistic value in terms of preliminary organization nd structure. The sketch always begins with the ead, drawn by means of an oval. Pass quickly om the head to the general shape of the figure, aaking corrections by drawing a new line without abbing anything out.

An idea of volume can also be given in the sketch: just give yourself plenty of room and emphasize light and shade by eliminating all the halftones. All this will be of use when painting the final picture. If you are drawing with a pencil, proceed as described, making sure to clearly mark the areas of shadow. If you draw with Indian ink, the

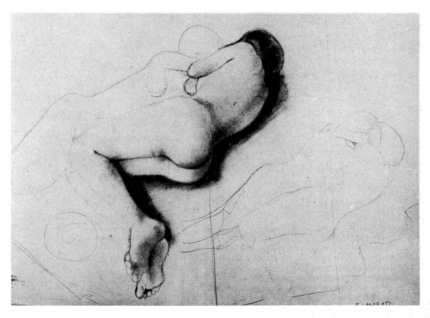

pposite: Felice Casorati: Sketch for Sleeping Girls, *1926 – rivate Collection, Turin*

Felice Casorati: Study of Nudes, *1926 – Private Collection, Turin*

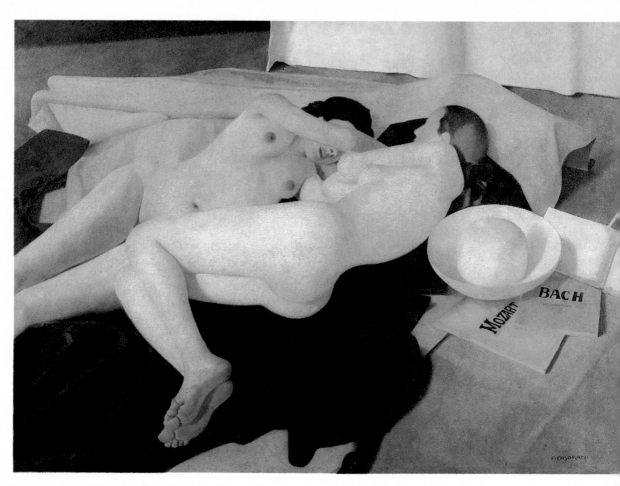

Felice Casorati: Sleeping Girls (Mozart), *1927 – 100 × 134.5 cm – Private Collection, Maranello*

results will be excellent from the point of view of
plasticity.

Using ink, remember that in addition to quill pens
and bamboo pens, any other kind of pointed instrument can be used. I have even made small
sketches with a toothpick. This was during the
period in which I was studying the cave drawings
in Val Camonica. I made small, synthetic drawings of the effects of shadow, which I later
reproduced on a larger scale. Abstract painting,
you see, also has to take account of the art of the
remote past. As I said before, a sketch must try to
capture the essentials and must never enter into
detail. A fat or thin figure in movement can be
rendered with just a few basic lines. When sketching, it is important to give an idea of character:
fat, thin, nervous, calm, short, tall, sitting, stand-

Francisco Goya (1746-1828): La Maja Vestida, *1801-1803 – oil on canvas, 95 × 190 cm – Prado, Madrid*

ing and so on. Two lines and some shading are often enough.

Goya's *Majas*

No visitor to the Prado, Spain's most important art gallery, would ever go away without having seen Francisco Goya's two famous *Majas*. These two paintings owe their fame partly to the fact that the naked woman is reputed to be the Duchess of Alba.

Critics, however, have proved this version of events to be incorrect, identifying the model as Pepita Tudo, a young Andalusian woman.

Francisco Goya: La Maja Desnuda, *1800 – oil on canvas, 97 × 190 cm – Prado, Madrid*

The *Maja Desnuda* was without doubt the most scandalous picture Goya ever painted. Goya had plenty of models on which to base his work. The pose he selected is almost certainly based on Titian's *Venus*. The nude was a popular subject in 16th century European painting. In Spain, however, with the exception of Velázquez's *Rokeby Venus*, nudes were hardly ever to be found. Goya's painting differs from the others (the sensuous nudes of Boucher or Fragonard, for example) in its realism.

It is likely that Goya was influenced by French painting, with which he was very familiar, though French nudes of the period tend to emphasize

eroticism rather than realism. Füssli's *Nude and Woman Playing the Harpsichord*, a variation on Titian's *Venus*, was painted in the same year as the *Maja Desnuda* and it is perhaps no coincidence that the two painters, who were so alike in many other ways should have based their works on the same model.

The *Maja Vestida* and the *Maja Desnuda* were put on show to the public only in 1901, one hundred years after being painted.

Above: Heinrich Füssli (1741-1825): Nude and Woman Playing the Harpsichord, *1799-1800 – oil on canvas, 71 × 91 cm – Offentliche Kunstsammlung, Basel*

Diego Velázquez (1599-1660): The Rokeby Venus, *1645-1648 – oil on canvas, 122.5 × 177 cm – National Gallery, London*

FRESCOS

Frescos are the most difficult kind of painting to paint. The great Goya desperately wanted to paint a fresco. There was a time when fresco painting was regarded as the most important kind of painting of all, but nowadays the art has almost died out. The word fresco is sometimes wrongly used to denote only large-scale paintings done by hand. How did painters learn how to paint frescos? How was the technique handed down from one generation to another?

First of all we have to say a few words about the "bottega d'arte" or the art schools of years ago. These were fascinating places where young, would-be artists were sent to learn their trade and where the most talented of them eventually became Masters. How exactly was a "bottega" organized? First there were the so-called "garzoni" or apprentices. These were boys from poor families aged from 5 to 9 who were given to the bottega in exchange for board and lodging. Their job was to keep the brushes in order, mix up the paints in the mortar with a pestle, carry the buckets of paint, sieve the sand, hand bowls of mixed paints to the pupils as they worked and generally stay at the side of the pupils and Masters ready to carry out all their requests. They learned to paint by watching the others and then became non-paying pupils or "boarders". Then there were the real pupils, boys of 11 to 13 years of age, whose families paid to send them to learn their trade at the bottega. Obviously it was in the Master's interests to find as many paying pupils as possible. The pupils normally performed easy tasks, such as painting the houses, trees or drapery in large pictures. They also helped the Master with the preparation of cartoons and paints.

Lastly, there were the "collaboratori" or assistants, older boys of about fifteen or so who were paid by the Master. They drew the cartoons, helped by the Master himself. Many of these boys would probably be Masters themselves when they were older. The Master was generally very demanding and had to be good at dealing with the spirit of competition that often grew up inside the bottega.

When pupils competed with one another, they often produced their best work. Michelangelo sculptured the *Madonna della Scala* when he was only 13 and Masaccio had already completed the frescos for which he is famous by the time of his death at the age of only 24. Sometimes the very best pupils surpassed even the Master in artistic skill.

Customers of the bottega, i.e. the men who

ordered the paintings or frescos and paid for them, always knew how well the Master and his pupils worked. Before any job was accepted, a detailed contract or deed had to be drawn up and signed in the presence of a notary. The deed contained the dates on which the work was to start and finish; the subject to be painted; a list of working days and rest days; the materials to be used (as specified by the Master), and details of board and lodging for the Master and his pupils, often including the kind of food they would eat. If the work was not finished on the specified date, the Master had to pay damages to the customer and had to pay for board and lodging for himself and his pupils for every extra day it took to finish the work.

If the subject being painted was a religious one, the Master was helped by a theologian whose job was to ensure that the painting gave a correct interpretation of the Bible or the Holy Scriptures. Once the Master had received the order and signed the contract, he had to study the subject, choose the models, prepare the cartoons, carry out the sinopie, check the tools and the materials, assign all the various tasks to his assistants, correct

Masolino da Panicale (ca. 1383-1440): Adam and Eve – *fresco – Carmine Church, Brancacci Chapel, Florence*

any mistakes made by the pupils, and paint the difficult parts such as the faces. The pupils in the bottega learned by example and by imitating the Master; if the Master was a very good painter, the pupils also became highly skilled. Pupils who worked with several Masters learned lots of different techniques and styles. They became far more versatile artists than those who had always worked in the same bottega or with the same Master.

In 1700 Father Ignazio Pozzo published his *Instructions* for painting on walls. He described the technique of fresco painting in the following way: "Make sure not to start painting until the plaster is in the condition where your fingers can make no impression on it." This was regarded by Father Pozzo and his contemporaries as the only valid technique for painting frescos. What he was really describing, though, was the technique known as 'mezzo-fresco,' since the real art of fresco painting had already been forgotten at the time his book was published.

In my opinion, the real fresco technique, which is much more difficult and very hard to learn, is by far the more beautiful. To paint a ceiling or a

Masaccio (1401-1428): Adam and Eve *(prior to restoration) – fresco – Carmine Church, Brancacci Chapel, Florence*

dome, you have to stay with your arms in a tiring and very uncomfortable position for days, weeks and sometimes months. You cannot afford to make mistakes. One error and you have to start all over again. When Vasari described fresco painting, the technique was already very different from that described by Cennino Cennini. In other words frescos in the time of Michelangelo were different from those painted by Cimabue. Prior to Cimabue fresco painting was a little known art. After Michelangelo it became 'mezzo-fresco,' as we have already seen. The end of fresco painting coincides with the advent of oil paints. Oil paints were easier to use and far more resistant to the elements.

What are the qualities needed by a good fresco painter? First of all, of course, he must be able to draw well and, the most important thing of all, he must be able to draw fast. Then he must be physically very strong because the work of preparing the plaster, putting it onto the wall and then smoothing it is basically the work of a labourer rather than of an artist.

There are various reasons why fresco painting is unlikely to come back into fashion nowadays. In the past buildings were built of solid brick and the walls were at least 70 cm thick. Nowadays hollow bricks are used; these are more practical and stronger but are not suitable for fresco painting because they dry very quickly. Another problem is the sand: it must be river sand gathered at points where the water runs slowly to make it fine and clean. But nowadays most of our rivers are polluted. The sand contains oxides and other chemical substances which would soon discolour the frescos.

The lime must be slaked for at least six months (a year would be even better) and prepared in small charcoal stoves (i.e. not industrial-type furnaces). Even supposing the right sand could be found, it would then have to be sieved and sorted into four different categories according to the size of the grains. The largest-grain sand is known as "arriccio" and is obtained by using a special arriccio sieve. The sand remaining in the sieve is sifted again through the 'mezzana' sieve, so that only the 'arriccio' remains. The sand is then passed through the 'mezzanina' sieve until only the 'mezzana' remains. This process goes on until all the sand has been sorted into the four different categories and placed into four different, appropriately labelled containers. This long and laborious job used to be carried out by the young apprentices in the bottega. Nowadays it is possible to use special sand-sifting machines.

Once sufficient quantities of each type of sand have been obtained, 2 parts of arricciato sand are mixed with 1 part of lime. A first layer is then applied with a trowel and smoothed with a plastering trowel. Leave it to dry for 10-20 minutes or until it adheres well to the wall. Then put on the second layer of plaster, obtained by mixing 2 parts of mezzana sand with 1 part of lime. Repeat these operations with the mezzanina sand and finally the fine sand, making four layers in all. At this point the cartoon is attached to the wall, after having been perforated with a needle or a pouncing roller. Powdered lampblack is applied to all the lines of the drawing by means of a special pad.

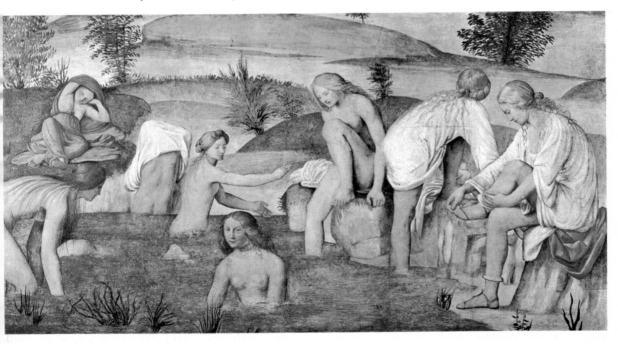

Bernardino Luini (1480/85-1532): Girls Bathing *(detail) – fresco from Pelucca – Brera Art Gallery, Milan*

Luca Signorelli (ca. 1445-1523): Resurrection of the Dead *(detail) – fresco – San Brizio Chapel, Orvieto Cathedral*

Opposite:
Raphael (1483-1520): La Galatea *– fresco – Villa della Farnesina, Rome*

When the cartoon is then removed, the drawing will have been transferred to the wall, in the form of tiny black dots like an embroidery pattern. Painting must begin while the wall is still wet, using soft, long-haired brushes (sometimes known as writing brushes).

Painting a fresco is a bit like painting in the dark since the colours you see as you are painting are not those that you will see when the fresco is dry. Fresco painters must therefore know exactly what the colours are going to look like when dry. Ultramarine blue, for example, will become a very pale, light blue when dry, unless there is a suitable protective coat underneath. This protective coat consists of a layer of burnt umber beneath the whole of the surface to be painted blue. All the different shades of yellow will also change as they dry. The only colours that do not change are the raw and burnt "earth" colours, dark reds and browns.

While painting the fresco, a piece of sacking cloth must be nailed to the wall and kept soaking wet with water at all times. The plaster will absorb the water and remain damp for as long as required. The lime, as Cennini says, "must be stirred until it has the consistency of ointment." The powder paints must be kept for two months in glass jars immersed in water. The powder is

Michelangelo Buonarroti (1475-1564): Ignudo
(detail over the prophet Isaiah), 1509 – fresco –
Sistine Chapel, Vatican City

taken out of the jars with a ladle just before starting the painting and mixed with water in an earthenware pot or bowl, using 4 parts of water to every 1 part of powder. The paint is then stirred continuously with a brush until it has the consistency of a good red wine. The paint must be put on quickly. There must be no wind or strong draughts and the temperature must be between 15 and 25°C.

All this general information is obviously meant only to give you an idea of the enormous difficulties artists had to face when painting frescos.

Goya learnt to paint frescos in Italy. Raphael called fresco painting "manly painting"; Cennini called it "the best painting there is"; Michelangelo painted the ceiling of the Sistine Chapel practically on his own; Leonardo da Vinci, knowing the speed at which he worked, didn't even bother to try.

Fresco painting and the bottega are unfortunately things of the past. I was lucky enough to study with one of the very last fresco painters. At school we painted only a few very small frescos but this was quite enough for me to be able to imagine the immense effort and torment suffered by painters like Tiepolo, Masaccio, Masolino or Piero della Francesca who had to work on frescos of enormous dimensions.

INDEX